Katie Wilkinson was called to the Bar in 2003, and has since practised as a Barrister. Katie specialises in consumer credit law, having been extensively involved in all of the well-publicised consumer arguments since 2006 including unfair bank charges, s.77-79 CCA 1974 requests, mis-sold insurance and investment products, s.140 unfair relationship claims, and secret commissions.

Katie has appeared routinely in unfair relationship claims relating to the sale of PPI, motor finance claims regarding the duties of car dealerships, and unfairness arising in the context of high value secured bridging loans. She also advises lenders and credit unions as to compliance issues affecting their contractual documentation.

Katie practises on the Midland Circuit at Halcyon Chambers, Birmingham.

A Practical Guide to Unfair Relationship Claims and Consumer Credit

A Practical Guide to Unfair Relationship Claims and Consumer Credit

Katie Wilkinson

Barrister, Lincoln's Inn

LLB (Hons)

Law Brief Publishing

Published 2025 by Law Brief Publishing, an imprint of Law Brief Publishing Ltd
30 The Parks
Minehead
Somerset
TA24 8BT

www.lawbriefpublishing.com

Paperback: 978-1-916698-93-2

PREFACE

Allegations of unfairness arising in the context of consumer agreements have featured in creditor/debtor disputes for decades and, following the commencement of the Consumer Credit Act 2006, the specific concept of 'unfair relationships' was recognised by way of the introduction of sections 140A-C into the Consumer Credit Act 1974.

Litigation based upon the unfair relationship provisions is now widespread. Quite often, unfairness is alleged in response to claims commenced by creditors for the purposes of enforcement, whilst at other times lawsuits are brought by the individual consumer in standalone claims issued against the lender. The scope of the unfair relationship provisions reaches far beyond consumer claims however, and the frequency of such allegations being raised in actions involving commercial/business borrowing is increasing exponentially.

To provide a conclusive answer as to the circumstances in which a court would uphold an allegation of unfairness would be an impossibility; the factual allegations of unfairness relied upon by borrowers are ever evolving, the remedies available to correct unfairness are extremely varied and, ultimately, any award is in the discretion of the court. As such, this book endeavours to highlight examples of the most common claims of unfairness that arise in consumer and non-consumer disputes, to identify the allegations that are most likely to succeed, and to recognise areas of anticipated growth.

It is intended that readers of this work will gain an insight into how the courts deal with claims of unfair relationship in practice, and will find a useful summary of the key issues that routinely arise.

All law is believed to be up to date as of 31 May 2025, and any errors are mine alone.

Katie Wilkinson
31 May 2025

CONTENTS

CHAPTER ONE

INTRODUCTION

The unfair relationship provisions found within sections 140A to 140C of the Consumer Credit Act 1974 provide a mechanism for unfairness to be identified as between a borrower and a creditor, and for such unfairness to be remedied by way of a range of court orders.

The wide scope of the provisions impacts a significant proportion of all credit agreements in existence, and also many that have ended. Awareness as to the existence of the unfair relationship provisions, and a significant increase in the number of borrowers bringing their complaints to the attention of the courts, has brought about rapid development to this area of law.

As readers of this text will learn, the unfair relationship provisions are extremely accessible and 'user-friendly' for borrowers. Allegations of unfairness have resulted in wide-scale mass litigation in fields such as the sale of insurance products linked to credit agreements, and motor finance agreements. In such cases, potential claimants are often actively encouraged by way of national TV and radio advertising campaigns to litigate claims against their creditors. In other cases, allegations of unfairness are made as part of a wider dispute. In actions where a creditor seeks repayment of loan sums and has issued a claim against a borrower, there is often much to be gained and little to be lost in pleading a claim of unfair relationship. At the very least, the court may find one aspect of unfairness proven which, in turn, could result in a financial benefit being awarded to the complainant.

Unfairness itself is not defined within the legislation and it is open to the court to scrutinise all aspects of the creditor/debtor relationship both before and after entry into a credit agreement. The actual express terms of the credit agreement itself may also be challenged on grounds of unfairness.

Given the broad discretion afforded by the legislation in applying the unfair relationship provisions, practitioners are often left with limited clarity as to how a court might deal with the complaints of unfairness alleged. The landscape is also constantly evolving, with new and often untested allegations of unfairness regularly advanced by borrowers.

Whilst successful unfair relationship claims can lead to remedies that are arguably severe against lenders, it is noteworthy that creditors have enjoyed their own successes in defending against unfairness allegations, even in cases where the operation of the credit agreements impact harshly on borrowers.

For anyone involved in advancing or defending an unfair relationship claim, it is essential to look to reported case law for insight into how the courts address – or are likely to address – claims of unfairness. Additionally, practitioners may find the many consumer-focused articles available online to be a helpful resource.

Many of the reported cases are referenced within this text, often more than once. Readers will find a degree of repetition in some of the content so that each chapter may be read independently without the need to cross refer to earlier sections of the book.

With ongoing developments in case law and a decision from the Supreme Court regarding motor finance agreements awaited, the landscape of unfair relationship claims will inevitably continue to unfold.

CHAPTER TWO

THE UNFAIR RELATIONSHIP PROVISIONS

The unfair relationship provisions are found at sections 140A, 140B and 140C of the Consumer Credit Act 1974, as amended. The provisions in force are set out below.

140A Unfair relationships between creditors and debtors

1) *The court may make an order under section 140B in connection with a credit agreement if it determines that the relationship between the creditor and the debtor arising out of the agreement (or the agreement taken with any related agreement) is unfair to the debtor because of one or more of the following–*

    a) *any of the terms of the agreement or of any related agreement;*

    b) *the way in which the creditor has exercised or enforced any of his rights under the agreement or any related agreement;*

    c) *any other thing done (or not done) by, or on behalf of, the creditor (either before or after the making of the agreement or any related agreement).*

2) *In deciding whether to make a determination under this section the court shall have regard to all matters it thinks relevant (including matters relating to the creditor and matters relating to the debtor).*

3) *For the purposes of this section the court shall (except to the extent that it is not appropriate to do so) treat anything done (or not done) by, or on behalf of, or in relation to, an associate or a former associate of the creditor as if done (or not done) by, or on behalf of, or in relation to, the creditor.*

4) *A determination may be made under this section in relation to a relationship notwithstanding that the relationship may have ended.*

5) *An order under section 140B shall not be made in connection with a credit agreement which is an exempt agreement for the purposes of Chapter 14A of Part 2 of the Regulated Activities Order by virtue of article 60C(2) of that Order (regulated mortgage contracts and regulated home purchase plans).*

6) *An order under section 140B shall not be made in connection with a credit agreement entered into under the Bounce Back Loan Scheme.*

7) *In subsection (6) "the Bounce Back Loan Scheme" means the scheme of that name operated from 4 May 2020 by the British Business Bank plc on behalf of the Secretary of State.*

140B Powers of court in relation to unfair relationships

1) *An order under this section in connection with a credit agreement may do one or more of the following–*

    a) *require the creditor, or any associate or former associate of his, to repay (in whole or in part) any sum paid by the debtor or by a surety by virtue of the agreement or any related agreement (whether paid to the creditor, the associate or the former associate or to any other person);*

b) require the creditor, or any associate or former associate of his, to do or not to do (or to cease doing) anything specified in the order in connection with the agreement or any related agreement;

c) reduce or discharge any sum payable by the debtor or by a surety by virtue of the agreement or any related agreement;

d) direct the return to a surety of any property provided by him for the purposes of a security;

e) otherwise set aside (in whole or in part) any duty imposed on the debtor or on a surety by virtue of the agreement or any related agreement;

f) alter the terms of the agreement or of any related agreement;

g) direct accounts to be taken, or (in Scotland) an accounting to be made, between any persons.

2) An order under this section may be made in connection with a credit agreement only–

a) on an application made by the debtor or by a surety;

b) at the instance of the debtor or a surety in any proceedings in any court to which the debtor and the creditor are parties, being proceedings to enforce the agreement or any related agreement; or

c) at the instance of the debtor or a surety in any other proceedings in any court where the amount paid or payable under the agreement or any related agreement is relevant.

3) *An order under this section may be made notwithstanding that its effect is to place on the creditor, or any associate or former associate of his, a burden in respect of an advantage enjoyed by another person.*

4) *An application under subsection (2)(a) may only be made–*

   a) *in England and Wales, to the county court;*

   b) *in Scotland, to the sheriff court;*

   c) *in Northern Ireland, to the High Court (subject to subsection (6)).*

5) *In Scotland such an application may be made in the sheriff court for the district in which the debtor or surety resides or carries on business.*

6) *In Northern Ireland such an application may be made to the county court if the credit agreement is an agreement under which the creditor provides the debtor with–*

   a) *fixed-sum credit not exceeding £15,000; or*

   b) *running-account credit on which the credit limit does not exceed £15,000.*

7) *Without prejudice to any provision which may be made by rules of court made in relation to county courts in Northern Ireland, such rules may provide that an application made by virtue of subsection (6) may be made in the county court for the division in which the debtor or surety resides or carries on business.*

8) *A party to any proceedings mentioned in subsection (2) shall be entitled, in accordance with rules of court, to have any person*

who might be the subject of an order under this section made a party to the proceedings.

9) *If, in any such proceedings, the debtor or a surety alleges that the relationship between the creditor and the debtor is unfair to the debtor, it is for the creditor to prove to the contrary.*

140C Interpretation of ss. 140A and 140B

1) *In this section and in sections 140A and 140B'credit agreement' means any agreement between an individual (the 'debtor') and any other person (the 'creditor') by which the creditor provides the debtor with credit of any amount.*

2) *References in this section and in sections 140A and 140B to the creditor or to the debtor under a credit agreement include–*

   a) *references to the person to whom his rights and duties under the agreement have passed by assignment or operation of law;*

   b) *where two or more persons are the creditor or the debtor, references to any one or more of those persons.*

3) *The definition of 'court' in section 189(1) does not apply for the purposes of sections 140A and 140B.*

4) *References in sections 140A and 140B to an agreement related to a credit agreement (the 'main agreement') are references to–*

   a) *a credit agreement consolidated by the main agreement;*

   b) *a linked transaction in relation to the main agreement or to a credit agreement within paragraph (a);*

c) *a security provided in relation to the main agreement, to a credit agreement within paragraph (a) or to a linked transaction within paragraph (b).*

5) *In the case of a credit agreement which is not a regulated consumer credit agreement, for the purposes of subsection (4) a transaction shall be treated as being a linked transaction in relation to that agreement if it would have been such a transaction had that agreement been a regulated consumer credit agreement.*

6) *For the purposes of this section and section 140B the definitions of 'security' and 'surety' in section 189(1) apply (with any appropriate changes) in relation to–*

   a) *a credit agreement which is not a consumer credit agreement as if it were a consumer credit agreement; and*

   b) *a transaction which is a linked transaction by virtue of subsection (5).*

7) *For the purposes of this section a credit agreement (the 'earlier agreement') is consolidated by another credit agreement (the 'later agreement') if–*

   a) *the later agreement is entered into by the debtor (in whole or in part) for purposes connected with debts owed by virtue of the earlier agreement; and*

   b) *at any time prior to the later agreement being entered into the parties to the earlier agreement included–*

      i. *the debtor under the later agreement; and*

      ii. *the creditor under the later agreement or an associate or a former associate of his.*

8) *Further, if the later agreement is itself consolidated by another credit agreement (whether by virtue of this subsection or subsection (7)), then the earlier agreement is consolidated by that other agreement as well.*

Section 140D was repealed by operation of The Financial Services and Markets Act 2000 (Regulated Activities) (Amendment) (No.2) Order 2013 (S.I. 2013/1881).

CHAPTER THREE

THE OLD REGIME, COMMENCEMENT OF THE NEW LEGISLATION, AND THE TRANSITIONAL PERIOD

The 'Old Regime' – Extortionate Credit Bargains

Legislation empowering the Court to reopen credit agreements existed long before the enactment of the unfair relationship provisions. Specifically, sections 137 to 139 of the Consumer Credit Act 1974 ('CCA 1974'), set out the provisions relating to 'extortionate credit bargains'.

Section 138(1) of the CCA 1974 declared a credit bargain to be extortionate if it:

> *(a) Requires the debtor or a relative of his to make payments (whether unconditionally, or on certain contingencies) which are grossly exorbitant, or*
>
> *(b) Otherwise grossly contravenes the principles of fair dealing.*

At sections 138(2) and (3), the court was required to have regard to evidence of prevailing interest rates at the time the credit bargain was made, and to evidence as to factors applicable to the debtor personally such as age, experience, business capacity, state of health, any issues of financial pressure, and the nature of that pressure.

The position of the creditor also fell to be considered under section 138(4). The court would consider a number of factors including the degree of risk accepted by the creditor in providing credit, whether any security had been provided, the creditor's relationship to the debtor, and whether or not a colourable cash price was quoted in the credit bargain for any goods and services provided.

Where a credit bargain was held to be extortionate, the credit agreement could be reopened at the discretion of the court (section 139). Thereafter the court could direct accounts to be taken, set aside any obligation imposed on the debtor, require a creditor to repay sums paid under the credit bargain, direct the return of any surety property, and/or alter the terms of the credit agreement or any security instrument.

Whilst the power of the court to alter the contractual position as between the parties was reasonably wide once an extortionate credit bargain had been identified, a debtor's success in such a claim was limited to establishing that the cost of borrowing was *'grossly exorbitant'* or that it did *'otherwise grossly contravene the ordinary principles of fair dealing'*. As a result, while the legislation provided some protection for debtors who had been financially exploited, it did not allow for the consideration of broader issues of unfairness in the creditor-debtor relationship.

The burden of proving that a credit bargain was *not* extortionate rested on the lender. However, despite this, for debtors who raised claims or defences of extortionate credit bargain, the narrow grounds upon which claim could succeed often meant that court ordered remedies were unobtainable.

The court acknowledged that the statutory test as to whether a credit bargain was 'extortionate' was a 'high one' in *Broadwick Financial Services Ltd v Spencer* [2002] EWCA Civ 35. In that case, Lord Justice Dyson discussed the potential inadequacy of the legislation, referring expressly to a report issued by the Director General of Fair Trading in September 1991. Within the report, entitled "Unjust Credit Transactions", concerns were expressed regarding the statutory test and the provisions of sections 137–140 of the CCA 1974. *Broadwick* noted that *"the report identified certain abuses affecting non-status borrowers in the secured lending market, and expressed the opinion that the extortionate credit bargain provisions of the Act had not dealt effectively with the problems to which they were addressed."*

The report recommended that the government introduce legislation *"to reform and develop sections 137–140 of the Consumer Credit Act, recasting them with a view to making them work as originally intended. The concept of an "unjust credit transaction" should replace that of an "extortionate credit bargain". In such cases the court would, as now, have the power to reopen an agreement, on application by the debtor (or surety), so as to do justice between the parties."*[1]

The complexity of the consumer legislation was also highlighted in *McGinn v Grangewood Securities Ltd* [2002] EWCA Civ 522. In the opening paragraph of the judgment, the '*unsatisfactory state of the law*' was acknowledged. The judgment went on to state that *"Simplification of a part of the law which is intended to protect consumers is surely long overdue so as to make it comprehensible to layman and lawyer alike. At present it is certainly not comprehensible to the former and is scarcely comprehensible to the latter"*.

The Consumer Credit Act 2006

Despite the perceived inadequacy of the legislation being a matter of concern since the early 1990's, the solution to these acknowledged shortcomings did not materialise until many years later with the enactment of the Consumer Credit Act 2006 (CCA 2006). At the time, the introduction of the CCA 2006 represented the most significant reform in consumer credit law since the CCA 1974 came into force. However, despite the Court of Appeal having identified a need for 'simplification' of the legislation in *McGinn*, the reform arguably triggered a sequence of major changes to consumer legislation which, over time, has resulted in an accumulation of layers of complexity.

---

1 See paragraph 1.9 of the Unjust Credit Transactions Report

The CCA 2006 came into force on 30 March 2006. Sections 19 to 22 amended the CCA 1974 by introducing sections 140A, 140B, 140C and 140D, better known as the 'unfair relationship' provisions. Section 140A empowered the court to declare the existence of an unfair relationship, whilst section 140B allowed the court to remedy unfairness by way of court order, at its discretion.[2] It was anticipated that the unfair relationship provisions would provide the courts with much more flexibility in determining both the existence of unfairness, and as to the range of orders that could be made by way of remedy.

The unfair relationship provisions themselves came into force at the later date of 6 April 2007. The legislation did not have retrospective effect, but would apply to all new and existing agreements, save for any agreements that became 'completed' during the transitional period.

The Transitional Period

The transitional provisions structured the implementation of the CCA 2006, specifying which parts of the legislation applied to credit agreements in effect before the unfair relationship provisions came into force, as well as to those agreements existing throughout the transitional period, and to agreements entered into once the transitional period had expired.

The transitional period commenced on 6 April 2007 and subsisted for one year. The intention behind the provisions was to allow creditors sufficient time to ensure that any agreements continuing beyond the end of the transitional period complied with the new legislation.

Paragraphs 14 to 16 of Schedule 3 to the CCA 2006 provide the provisions relevant to claims of unfair relationship. Paragraph 14(1)

2 Section 140C provides interpretation of s140A and 140B, and section 140D provided 'advice and information'.

provides that a court can only make a section 140B order[3] in respect of an agreement made before 6 April 2007 if the debtor's application for a declaration of unfairness was made after the expiry of the transitional period (paragraph 14(4)).

Paragraph 14(2) of schedule 3 provides that *'the court shall not make'* an order under the unfair relationship provisions if the agreement in question becomes a completed agreement prior to 6 April 2007 or becomes competed during the transitional period.

Completed Agreements

Paragraph 1(2) of schedule 3 provides that an agreement becomes a completed agreement once both of the following conditions are met:

- There is no sum payable under the agreement.
- There is no sum which will, or may, become so payable.

Whilst the description of what constitutes a 'completed agreement' may at first appear straight forward, it has been the subject of considerable dispute. Complexity arose in agreements which included 'linked' transactions, most notably in cases involving optional insurance products such as Payment Protection Insurance (PPI). In such agreements the PPI policy would be 'linked' to the main agreement. If a borrower entered into a personal loan agreement and took out a PPI policy, but later cancelled the policy while keeping the loan, the completion date of the linked transaction would differ from the completion date of the loan agreement. If an unfair relationship claim was brought on the basis of unfairness arising from the sale of the PPI policy only, there was an identifiable argument that the PPI agreement had in fact completed either before or during the transitional period. If that argument was

3 An Order to remedy established unfairness under s.140A

correct, the unfair relationship claim would not be available to the borrower.

The dispute on this issue culminated in a binding decision from the Supreme Court in *Smith and another v Royal Bank of Scotland* [2023] UKSC 34. Pivotally, the Supreme Court held that where a linked transaction completed before or during the transitional period, an unfair relationship claim could still be brought in relation to that linked transaction so long as the underlying credit agreement subsisted beyond the end of the transitional period.

Summary

The unfair relationship provisions apply to all relevant credit agreements that were either:

a) entered into after 6 April 2008;

b) entered into before 6 April 2007 but subsisted beyond 6 April 2008; or

c) entered into during the transitional period of 6 April 2007 to 6 April 2008, and subsisted beyond its end date.

The effect of the transitional provisions as set out at schedule 3 paragraph 14 of CCA 2006 is that the court *may* make an order under section 140B in connection with all credit agreements entered into *after* 5 April 2007, but for credit agreements which existed since *before* the commencement of the unfair relationship provisions (6 April 2007), an order could only be made if the unfair relationship claim was brought after expiry of the one-year transitional period. If the agreement completed at any point prior to the commencement of the legislation or during the one-year transitional period, the unfair relationship provisions are simply unavailable to borrowers.

CHAPTER FOUR

SCOPE OF THE UNFAIR RELATIONSHIP PROVISIONS

The old regime of 'extortionate credit bargain'[4] applied to credit agreements generally. In the same way, section 140A of the CCA 1974 permits a court to make an order under section 140B *'in connection with a credit agreement'*. When coming into force, the unfair relationship provisions therefore encompassed any agreement entered into between a creditor and an individual or small partnership. The unfair relationship provisions were available to debtors even in circumstances where the agreement in question would otherwise be 'exempt' under the CCA 1974.

There were a number of early reported cases involving borrowing for business purposes. While such agreements would typically be exempt under the CCA 1974, the broad scope of the unfair relationship provisions meant that allegations of unfairness were still subject to consideration should a claim be made. Consequently, the number of reported cases that involve non-consumer disputes has grown significantly.

Some restrictions on the use of the unfair relationship provisions have since been imposed following The Mortgage Credit Directive (*2014/17/EU*) (MCD) regime which came into force on 21 March 2016. The Directive brought about a change in regulation for certain agreements from the CCA 1974 to the Financial Conduct Authority mortgage regime. Section 140A(5) CCA 1974 expressly excludes from the unfair relationship provisions any credit agreement that is an 'exempt agreement' for the purposes of Chapter 14A of Part 2 of the Financial

---

4 Sections 137 to 170 CCA 1974

Services and Markets Act 2000 (Regulated Activities) Order 2001[5] by virtue of article 60C(2), which deals with regulated mortgage contracts and regulated home purchase plans. The following agreements are therefore now excluded from the scope of the unfair relationship provisions:

- Agreements secured by land mortgages where entry into the agreement as a creditor is a regulated activity for the purposes of the FSMA.[6]

- Agreements that are, or form part of, a regulated "home purchase plan" where entering into the agreement as home purchase provider is a regulated activity for the purposes of the FSMA.

The unfair relationship provisions do not, therefore, apply to regulated mortgage contracts or home purchase plans, but do apply to other exempt agreements.

Section 140A(6) CCA 1974 also expressly excludes agreements provided under the Bounce Back Loan Scheme.[7] This scheme is defined at section 140A(7) as being *"the scheme of that name operated from 4 May 2020 by the British Business Bank plc on behalf of the Secretary of State"*, being the finance agreements made available as support for businesses during the Covid-19 pandemic.

---

5 SI 2001/544

6 Financial Services and Markets Act 2000

7 Sections 140A(6) and (7) were inserted (retrospective to 4 May 2020) by the Business and Planning Act 2020

Linked Agreements

Section 140A(1) of the CCA 1974 requires the court not only to consider the credit agreement itself, but to also consider that agreement "taken with any related agreement". Section 140C(4) explains that references to an agreement related to the "main agreement" are references to:

a) a credit agreement consolidated by the main agreement;

b) a "linked transaction" in relation to the main agreement/an agreement within paragraph (a); and

c) a security provided in relation to the main agreement or agreements failing within (a) and (b).

A credit agreement that is consolidated by a main agreement might include circumstances where a debtor refinances his debts. An unfair relationship claim brought in relation to the main agreement may require the court to look at any number of earlier agreements that were effectively redeemed by entry into the main agreement.

A description as to what constitutes a 'linked transaction' is found in section 19 CCA 1974. Whilst the word 'transaction' is not given a specific definition, a 'transaction' is plainly different to an 'agreement', and is wider in its scope. A linked transaction may also be a credit or hire agreement in its own right. In broad terms, a transaction will be a 'linked transaction' to the credit agreement in relation to the main agreement if, among other factors, it is an agreement entered into by the debtor with the creditor, the creditor initiated the transaction by way of suggesting it to the debtor, and the purpose of the linked transaction is related to the principal agreement.

Any security given by a debtor is expressly included as a related agreement for the purposes of assessing fairness.

Agreements at an End

Subject to any applicable limitation periods,[8] debtors can bring a claim of unfair relationship even in relation to credit agreements that have ended. While such agreements may have been fully repaid, the court is not precluded from reopening the credit agreement if an unfair relationship is found to exist.

Third Parties

Section 140A(1)(c) of the CCA 1974 extends to actions, or inaction/omissions, carried out on behalf of the creditor. As a result, the unfair relationship provisions apply to things done, or not done by third parties who are not themselves explicitly named within a credit agreement. This includes the creditor's employees and agents, brokers and credit intermediaries, debt recovery agencies instructed by the lender, and parties to related agreements.

Summary

The scope of the unfair relationship provisions is extremely broad, extending to all consumer credit agreements with individuals and small partnerships irrespective of the size of the loan or credit provided. These provisions apply to regulated credit agreements and most 'exempt' agreements, as well as agreements entered into by borrowers for business purposes.

However, certain agreements are excluded from being assessed for unfairness under section 140A of the CCA 1974, including regulated land mortgages, home purchase plans, and loans taken out under the 'Bounce Back Loan Scheme'.

---

8 See Chapter 5 – Limitation Periods for further discussion.

When considering whether a credit agreement is unfair, the court may examine any related agreements. These include earlier agreements that have been consolidated by the main agreement, any "linked transaction", and any security provided in connection with the main agreement. The actions (or inactions) of third parties in the transaction all fall to be considered.

Moreover, credit agreements can be reopened by the court even if they have concluded – whether through repayment or otherwise – subject to any issues of limitation.

CHAPTER FIVE

APPLYING FOR A DECLARATION AND THE BURDEN OF PROOF

Applying for a Declaration of Unfairness

Section 140B(2) of the CCA 1974 specifies who is eligible to apply for a declaration as to the existence of an unfair relationship and to seek an order remedying such unfairness.

An order may only be made in connection with a credit agreement in the following circumstances:

- On an application made by the debtor or by a surety – section 140B(2)(a)
- At the instance of the debtor or a surety in any proceedings in any court to which the debtor and the creditor are parties, being proceedings to enforce the agreement or any related agreement – section 140B(2)(b); or
- At the instance of the debtor or a surety in any other proceedings in any court where the amount paid or payable under the agreement or any related agreement is relevant – section 140B(2)(c)

Debtors are therefore able to make a standalone application seeking a declaration of unfair relationship, or can advance a defence and counterclaim alleging unfairness in response to a claim whereby the creditor is seeking to enforce a credit agreement or any related agreement, or where there exist proceedings relating to sums paid or payable under the agreement/any related agreement

Pursuant to section 140B(4), claims must be commenced as follows:

- England and Wales – the application must be made in the county court
- Scotland – the application can only be made to the sheriff court
- Northern Ireland – the application may be made to the High Court or to the county court provided certain conditions are met.

Burden of proof

The burden of proof is expressly reversed under section 140B(9) such that once an allegation of unfairness is raised by the borrower, it is for the creditor to prove on the balance of probabilities that the relationship is not unfair.

In practice, both borrowers and creditors often fall short in meeting the required standards for pleadings and evidence in unfair relationship claims. Borrowers seeking declarations under section 140A will frequently allege unfairness, but will then fail to adequately plead the particular circumstances said to give rise to that unfairness. In such cases the claim should not succeed, as the reversal of the burden of proof does not relieve a debtor of the usual requirement to particularise their allegations of unfairness. On the other hand, lenders often fall into the trap of offering a bare denial as to any unfairness arising. Such an approach is insufficient; lenders must provide detailed evidence in rebuttal of the allegations if a finding of unfairness is to be avoided.

In relation to evidence, each party bears the burden of proving their own asserted facts, as per *Promontoria (Henrico) Ltd v Samra* [2019] EWHC 2327 (Ch) at [24].[9]

[9] Approved by the Supreme Court in *Smith v RBS Plc* [2023] UKSC 34

CHAPTER SIX

LIMITATION PERIODS

Disputes over the application of the Limitation Act 1980 ('LA 1980') to unfair relationship claims arose shortly after the provisions came into force. While case law began to clarify aspects of the position as early as 2009, uncertainty persisted—particularly in relation to agreements linked to main credit agreements—until the issue was conclusively addressed by the Supreme Court in October 2023.

This chapter discusses the main issues that arise in claims affected by the LA 1980, and highlights the key case law relevant to those issues.

<u>Patel v Patel [2009] EWHC 3264</u>

The applicable limitation period for claims seeking a declaration of unfair relationship was first considered in detail in the High Court case of *Patel v Patel* [2009] EWHC 3264 (QB).

The factual background of *Patel* was that the parties had known each other for over 50 years and were family friends. There was no factual dispute that, beginning in 1979, the claimant had advanced sums totalling £56,450 to the defendant through a series of oral loan agreements. The claimant asserted that the final oral agreement, made in 1992, consolidated the earlier loans on terms that interest would accrue at a rate of 20% per annum, compounded monthly, with full repayment to be made upon request.

The claimant sought £207,465 as the estimated total amount outstanding in 1992, plus an amount which represented the compound interest that had accrued on that sum over the subsequent years.

The value of the claim at the time of issue was £4,556,181 and had grown to over £6 million by the time of trial.

The defendant partially defended the claim on grounds that the agreement gave rise to an unfair relationship under section 140A CCA 1974 and an order remedying the alleged unfairness was sought under section 140B.

The claimant argued that the defendant's application for relief under s.140B was time-barred by virtue of section 8 of the LA 1980 which reads:

Section 8(1):

> *"An action upon a specialty shall not be brought after the expiration of twelve years from the date on which the cause of action accrued."*

The defendant agreed that a claim of unfair relationship was indeed an action on a specialty to which section 8 of the LA 1980 applied, but the parties did not agree as to when that time period began. The claimant contended that the applicable twelve-year limitation period began to run from the date that the agreement was entered into.

In rejecting the claimant's argument, Leggatt QC (as he then was) stated at [62]:

> *"It seems to me that it would be a serious flaw in the legislation if the claimant were correct that the time limit for seeking an order under s.140B expires 12 years after the credit agreement giving rise to an unfair relationship was entered into. This would mean that in cases where unfairness to the debtor has persisted for a sufficient length of time, including cases where the very length of time that the creditor has waited before taking steps to enforce the agreement is itself a cause of unfairness, the court would be powerless to grant relief."*

The court identified the following critical question to be answered in unfair relationship claims:

> *"what is the relevant date at which the fairness or otherwise of the relationship has to be determined?"*[10]

The court held that the determination of whether an unfair relationship exists must be made by considering the entirety of the relationship and all potentially relevant factors up to the point of assessment. If the relationship between the creditor and debtor had ended, the relevant date for determining unfairness was the date the relationship concluded. However, if the relationship was ongoing, the assessment should be made as at the time of trial.

Since the defendant sought to recover sums pursuant to a section 140B order, the twelve-year limitation period under section 8 did not apply. Instead, the relevant provision of the LA 1980 was section 9, which sets out that the time limit for actions for sums recoverable by statute *"shall not be brought after the expiration of six years from the date on which the cause of action accrued."*

The key question, therefore, is when does the cause of action accrue? In *Patel*, the court held that the cause of action arises once all the material facts necessary to support an application under section 140B have come into existence. Those facts are, firstly, the existence of a credit agreement between the creditor and debtor, and secondly, that the relationship arising from that agreement is unfair to the debtor.[11]

The court concluded that the debtor's cause of action is a continuing one, accruing day by day until the relevant relationship comes to an end. It was held that *"an application under s.140B can be made at any time during the currency of the relationship arising out of a credit agreement, based on an*

---

10 See *Patel v Patel* at [65]

11 See *Patel v Patel* at [66]

allegation that the relationship is unfair to the debtor at the time when the application is made, or at any later time (as s.140A(4) expressly permits) until the expiration of the applicable period of limitation after the relationship has ended. (That period is 12 years except in so far as the relief sought is the recovery of money which has been paid by the debtor, in which case the effect of s.8(2) is that the six period prescribed by s.9(1) of the Limitation Act applies.)"[12]

Accordingly, the limitation defence was dismissed, and the defendant's claim of unfair relationship was held not to be time-barred.

Linked Transactions – *Smith v RBS* [2023] UKSC 34

Until the Supreme Court delivered its decision in *Smith v RBS*, the prevailing approach among practitioners and the courts was to assess limitation periods for 'linked transactions' by reference to the date the linked transaction was completed, rather than the completion date of the main agreement.

Smith v RBS involved appeals in two claims where the claimants sought declarations of unfairness and related remedies under the unfair relationship provisions, concerning the sale of payment protection insurance ('PPI'). Both claimants had entered into credit card agreements with RBS and had additionally agreed to take out PPI provided by third-party insurers. These insurers paid RBS commissions for selling the PPI, with the commission payments exceeding 50% of the value of the premiums paid. RBS did not disclose the existence or the value of these commission payments to the claimants.

Both claimants had made complaints to the bank pre-litigation and had accepted redress in accordance with the Financial Conduct Authority's

12 See *Patel v Patel* at [66]

DISP App 3 guidance.[13] That guidance required lenders to assess whether the sale of PPI was conducted fairly and provide redress in certain circumstances. As per the FCA redress scheme, each claimant was refunded all commission paid which exceeded 50% of the premium value, together with any related contractual interest and fees, and compensatory interest at 8% per annum.

The claimants subsequently pursued claims seeking repayment of all amounts they had paid in relation to the PPI policies, along with compensatory interest.

By the time the claims were issued, more than six years had elapsed since the PPI policies had ended. However, the credit card agreements remained in effect despite the cancellation of the PPI, and the claims were initiated within six years of the credit card agreements' termination.

RBS put forward two key arguments challenging the claimants' ability to rely on the unfair relationship provisions:

(i) The claims were statute barred;

(ii) The unfair relationship provisions were not available as the PPI policies had come to an end either before, or during the transitional period. Thus, they were 'completed' agreements.

Given that the claimants were seeking to reclaim sums already paid by them, the relevant limitation period was section 9 of the LA 1980.

At first instance, the claims were held not to be statute barred. However, on appeal, the Court of Appeal ruled in favour of the bank, determining that the alleged unfair relationship ended on the date the PPI policy concluded—more than six years prior to the claims being issued.

---

13 An appendix to the FCA Handbook which sets out the complaint handling process in relation to unfairness.

The Supreme Court thereafter unanimously allowed the appeals in favour of the customers.

The Supreme Court rejected RBS's argument that, where PPI policies were cancelled before the end of the transitional period, the unfair relationship provisions no longer applied because the policy was a 'completed' agreement. The Court held that cancellation of the PPI prior to the conclusion of the transitional period did not bar the court from assessing the unfairness of the ongoing credit agreement that financed the policy.

Given that the overarching credit card agreements remained in effect within six years of the claims being issued, the Supreme Court held that the claims were not statute-barred. The cause of action had not accrued—and therefore the six-year limitation period had not begun—until the credit relationship itself had ended.

The practical effect of the decision was significant: banks could no longer rely on limitation defences in cases where PPI policies had ended historically, typically due to cancellation by customers. For limitation purposes, time begins to run from the end of the overall credit relationship, even where PPI payments had ceased much earlier. Furthermore, banks could no longer argue that the unfair relationship provisions were inapplicable to PPI policies that had concluded prior to the transitional period, provided the overarching credit agreement remained active beyond that period.

<u>Section 32 Limitation Act 1980</u>

It is not uncommon for PPI unfair relationship claims to be brought even where more than six years have elapsed since the conclusion of the entire credit relationship. In such cases, it is typically accepted that the primary limitation period under section 9 of the LA 1980 has expired. In an attempt to disapply the primary limitation period, debtors often rely on section 32 which reads as follows:

32.— Postponement of limitation period in case of fraud, concealment or mistake.

1) Subject to subsections (3), (4A) and (4B) below, where in the case of any action for which a period of limitation is prescribed by this Act, either—

(a) the action is based upon the fraud of the defendant; or

(b) any fact relevant to the plaintiff's right of action has been deliberately concealed from him by the defendant; or

(c) the action is for relief from the consequences of a mistake;

the period of limitation shall not begin to run until the plaintiff has discovered the fraud, concealment or mistake (as the case may be) or could with reasonable diligence have discovered it. References in this subsection to the defendant include references to the defendant's agent and to any person through whom the defendant claims and his agent.

2) For the purposes of subsection (1) above, deliberate commission of a breach of duty in circumstances in which it is unlikely to be discovered for some time amounts to deliberate concealment of the facts involved in that breach of duty.[14]

Section 32 of the LA 1980 allows for the postponement of the standard limitation period in cases involving fraud, deliberate concealment, or mistake. Where a fact relevant to the claimant's right of action has been deliberately concealed by the defendant, the limitation period does not begin to run until the claimant has discovered the concealment—or could, with reasonable diligence, have discovered it.[15]

---

[14] Irrelevant parts of s.32 Limitation Act 1980 have been omitted.

[15] Section 32(1)(b) Limitation Act 1980

Section 32(2) expressly states that the deliberate commission of a breach of duty in circumstances where the breach is unlikely to be discovered for some time will amount to a deliberate concealment of the facts that are involved in that breach of duty.

A claimant wishing to rely on section 32(1)(b) to defeat a limitation defence must prove that there was a fact relevant to the claimant's right of action which was deliberately concealed from him by the defendant or his agent.

Consideration as to the application of section 32 begins with the Supreme Court's decision in *Plevin v Paragon Personal Finance Ltd* [2014] UKSC 61. In that case, the Court held that the non-disclosure of commission paid or retained in connection with the sale of a PPI policy could, in itself, give rise to an unfair relationship under section 140A of the Consumer Credit Act 1974—even though, at the time, there was no regulatory obligation requiring lenders to disclose such commissions to borrowers. Crucially, the finding of unfairness was made in the absence of any actual breach of regulatory duty.

In light of section 32(2) of the LA 1980—which provides that the deliberate commission of a breach of duty in circumstances where discovery is unlikely for some time amounts to deliberate concealment—this raised important questions. Specifically, whether a lender's failure to disclose commission could amount to "deliberate concealment," despite there being no formal duty of disclosure at the time of the transaction.

<u>*Canada Square Operations Ltd v Potter* [2020] EWHC 672 (QB)</u>

The issues surrounding deliberate concealment and the application of section 32 were firstly considered by the High Court in *Canada Square Operations Ltd v Potter*. The facts of the case closely mirrored those in *Plevin*. In 2006, Mrs Potter entered into a loan agreement with Canada Square, then trading as Egg Banking plc. Simultaneously, she purchased a PPI policy underwritten by a third-party insurer. Egg Banking received a commission from the insurer amounting to over 95% of the premiums paid under the policy.

Prior to the litigation, Canada Square had paid compensation to Mrs Potter but the amount of the compensation represented only a proportion of the sums paid by her in relation to the PPI policy.

The claim sought repayment of the remaining PPI premiums and associated interest on grounds of an unfair relationship existing. At first instance, the court found that the expired six-year primary limitation period should be disapplied. Having considered sections 32(1)(b) and 32(2) of the LA 1980, it was held that the non-disclosure of the commission had been deliberate and that Mrs Potter could not have ascertained the true position with reasonable diligence. Consequently, the primary limitation period was disapplied and Mrs Potter was permitted to rely on section 32.

Canada Square appealed the decision to the Court of Appeal.

Canada Square Operations Ltd v Potter [2021] EWCA 339

On appeal, Canada Square argued that the trial court had erred in two key respects: first, in finding that any relevant "duty" existed under section 32 of the LA 1980 to disclose the existence or extent of the commission; and second, in inferring that Canada Square knew, or should be taken to have known, that its failure to disclose such information amounted to a breach of duty.

The appeal was dismissed. The court held that Canada Square *was* under a relevant duty for the purposes of section 32(2) to disclose the existence and/or extent of the commission paid or retained from the PPI premiums. That duty, and the breach of it, arose not from the general law, but specifically from the statutory unfair relationship regime set out in sections 140A to 140D of the CCA 1974. The non-disclosure of the commission was found to be unfair and thus constituted a breach of that statutory duty.

The court further concluded that the concealment was deliberate within the meaning of section 32(2) of the LA 1980. The crucial factor was the existence and amount of the undisclosed commission. Canada Square had made a conscious decision not to disclose this information to Mrs Potter. It was held that Canada Square must be taken to have known it was under a duty to act fairly and had deliberately chosen to withhold disclosure of the commission—thereby satisfying the threshold for deliberate concealment.

In its conclusion, the Court of Appeal stated at [161]:

> *"Canada Square deliberately concealed from her a fact, namely the existence and extent of the commission they received, that fact being relevant to her right of action under section 140A. The period of limitation did not therefore begin to run on her claim under section 140A until she discovered the concealment in November 2018. Further or alternatively she can rely on section 32(1)(b) as expanded by section 32(2) because Canada Square deliberately committed a breach of their duty towards her under section 140A in circumstances where that breach was unlikely to be discovered for some time."*

Canada Square appealed to the Supreme Court.

Canada Square Operations Ltd v Potter [2023] UKSC 41

In its appeal, Canada Square sought clarification from the Supreme Court regarding the proper interpretation of the phrases 'deliberately concealed' in section 32(1)(b) and 'deliberate commission of a breach of duty' in section 32(2) of the LA 1980, in the context of determining whether Mrs Potter's claim was statute-barred.

The Supreme Court adopted a straightforward approach, giving the term 'concealment' its ordinary and natural meaning. Lord Reed stated at [98]:

> *"...the word 'conceal' means to keep something secret, either by taking active steps to hide it, or by failing to disclose it. A person who hides something can properly be described as concealing it, whether there is an obligation to disclose it or not."*

Concealment can thus be established by withholding information from another party, whether through active deception or passive omission. The claimant is not required to prove that the defendant owed a legal, moral, or social duty to disclose the information, nor must the claimant demonstrate that the defendant knew the fact was relevant to the claimant's right of action. What matters is that the defendant deliberately prevented the claimant from becoming aware of the fact, thereby obstructing the claimant's ability to initiate proceedings within the ordinary limitation period.

In considering what was meant by 'deliberate', Lord Reed stated at [109]:

> *"What is required is (1) a fact relevant to the claimant's right of action, (2) the concealment of that fact from her by the defendant, either by a positive act of concealment or by a withholding of the relevant information, and (3) an intention on the part of the defendant to conceal the fact or facts in question."*

The Supreme Court rejected the Court of Appeal's interpretation of 'deliberately' and instead adopted a more straightforward approach, consistent with the earlier Court of Appeal decision in *Williams v Fanshaw Porter and Hazelhurst (a firm)* [2004] EWCA Civ 157. At [108] Lord Reed stated:

> *"Accordingly, as Park J stated in Williams at para 14, the defendant must have considered whether to inform the claimant of the relevant fact and decided not to. So construed, section 32(1)(b) strikes a balance between the interests of the claimant and the defendant, as Parliament*

> *intended. If the defendant has concealed a fact from the claimant, and has done so deliberately, that is to say knowingly, then he has the means to start the limitation period running by disclosing the fact."*

It follows, therefore, that the mere non-disclosure of a fact may not be deliberate. There must have been consideration as to whether to disclose it, and a decision taken not to.

The Supreme Court also rejected the Court of Appeal's view that recklessness sufficed to establish deliberate breach of duty. It was stated at [153]:

> *"For all these reasons, the reasoning of the Court of Appeal in relation to section 32(2) cannot be accepted. 'Deliberate', in section 32(2), does not include 'reckless'. Nor does it include awareness that the defendant is exposed to a claim. As Lord Scott said in Cave at para 58, the words 'deliberate commission of a breach of duty' are clear words of English. They mean, as he added at para 61, that the defendant 'knows he is committing a breach of duty'."*

As to whether Canada Square's failure to disclose the existence and amount of the commission was a 'deliberate breach of duty' for the purposes of section 32(2), the Supreme Court held that it was not. Whilst the Court of Appeal had found there had been a breach of the duty arising under s.140 CCA 1976, the Supreme Court declined to find that the breach had been deliberate. It was held that a claimant who wishes to rely on section 32(2) must show that the defendant <u>knew</u> it was committing a breach of duty <u>or intended</u> to commit a breach of duty. It had not been shown that Canada Square knew or intended that its failure to disclose the commission to Mrs Potter would render their relationship unfair within the meaning of section 140A. Accordingly, Canada Square's breach of duty was not deliberate.

Mrs Potter was therefore able to rely upon section 32(1) of the Limitation Act 16980 to disapply the primary limitation period, but she was unable to rely upon section 32(2).

Reasonable Diligence

Claimants seeking to rely on section 32 often present evidence regarding when they first discovered the 'concealed' fact, but frequently neglect to address the critical issue of reasonable diligence as required by section 32(2). This omission can be fatal to an otherwise strong case, since under section 32 the limitation period does not begin until the claimant has discovered the fraud, concealment, or mistake—or could have discovered it with reasonable diligence. The burden rests on the claimant to prove that they could not, even with reasonable diligence, have uncovered the concealment any earlier.

Reasonable diligence was considered in *Paragon Finance v DB Thakerar & Co* [1999] 1 All ER 400 wherein Millet LJ stated:

> *"The question is not whether the plaintiffs should have discovered the fraud sooner; but whether they could with reasonable diligence have done so. The burden of proof is upon them. They must establish that they could not have discovered the fraud without exceptional measures which they could not reasonably have been expected to take...the test was how a person carrying on a business of the relevant kind would act if he had adequate but not unlimited staff and resources and was motivated by reasonable but not excessive sense of urgency."*

In *OT Computers Limited (in liquidation) v Infineon Technologies AG and Micron Europe Limited* [2021] EWCA Civ 501, the Court of Appeal recognised that, in some cases, discovery of the relevant facts occurs gradually as pieces of information emerge over time, making it difficult to pinpoint the exact 'date of knowledge'. The court also held that *"...personal traits or characteristics bearing on the likelihood of the particular claimant discovering facts which a person in his position could reasonably be expected to discover, such as whether the claimant is slothful, naïve, shy, nervous, uncurious or ill informed, are not relevant"*[16].

---

16 See *OT Computers* at [38]

In the more recent case of *Super Fast Trading Limited v The Governor and Company of the Bank of Ireland and another* [2025] EWHC 871 (Comm), *OT Computers* was considered in relation as to whether there had been a 'trigger event' which put the claimant on notice of a need to investigate. The court concluded that the timing of the trigger depends on the specific facts and circumstances of each case, and it should consider whether there was *"something which would have caused a reasonably attentive and diligent person to ask questions"*.[17]

Summary

Unfair relationship claims are classified as actions on a specialty, subject to a 12-year limitation period under section 8 of the Limitation Act 1980. However, where the claim seeks the return of money, a 6-year limitation period applies under section 9, which provides the limitation period for actions for sums recoverable by statute.

The primary limitation period begins from the end date of the unfair agreement, even if the alleged unfairness arises from a linked agreement that ended at an earlier date.

A claimant may disapply the primary limitation period by relying on section 32 of the Limitation Act 1980, which allows for postponement if any fact relevant to the claim has been deliberately concealed, and the claimant could not have discovered it earlier with reasonable diligence.

[17] See *Super Fast Trading Limited* at [80] and [82].

CHAPTER SEVEN

UNFAIR RELATIONSHIP PRINCIPLES

The unfair relationship provisions were introduced to give the courts greater flexibility to address unfairness arising from credit agreements between lenders and debtors—marking a significant departure from the more limited powers available under the earlier 'extortionate credit bargain' provisions. While the term "unfair relationship" is not expressly defined in section 140 of the Consumer Credit Act 1974 or elsewhere in the Act, the legislation does set out in general terms the types of conduct and circumstances which *may* give rise to an unfair relationship.

Having been drafted in extremely wide terms, section 140A(1) of the CCA 1974 allows the court to make an order under section 140B if it determines that the relationship between the creditor and the debtor is unfair because of one or more of the following:

- Any of the terms of the agreement or of any related agreement.

- The way in which the creditor has exercised or enforced any of their rights under the agreement or any related agreement.

- Any other thing done (or not done) by, or on behalf of, the creditor (either before the making of the agreement or any related agreement).

If there were any doubt as to whether section 140A(1) provides sufficient protection for borrowers, an even wider power can be found in section 140A(2) which states that the court *"shall have regard to all matters it thinks relevant"* in assessing the fairness of the relationship.

The Supreme Court provided definitive guidance on the operation of the unfair relationship provisions in the landmark case of *Plevin v Paragon Personal Finance Ltd* [2014] UKSC 61. Despite being handed down over a decade ago, the decision remains central to the analysis of all unfair relationship claims.

The factual narrative in *Plevin* was relatively typical of the many PPI complaints that were advancing through the court system at that time. Mrs Plevin wished to consolidate and refinance her financial liabilities. She retained the services of an independent credit broker who arranged a refinance loan with Paragon Personal Finance Ltd and who, at the same time, sold her a policy of PPI at a cost of £5,780.00. The PPI was a 'single premium' policy payable at the outset and added to loan. What Mrs Plevin did not know was that the premium charged consisted of a commission payable by Paragon to her credit broker. The value of that commission was 71.8% of the total cost of the premium.

Mrs Plevin brought a claim against Paragon. In it, she pleaded a case of unfair relationship based on a number of factors including a failure to advise on the suitability of the PPI for her individual needs and, pivotally, owing to the non-disclosure of the amount of the commission partially retained by Paragon and partially paid to her credit broker.[18]

The case advanced all the way to the Supreme Court who found in favour of Mrs Plevin. The relationship arising from the credit agreement was held to be unfair because the commission paid by Paragon to the credit broker was so large that it was unfair that Mrs Plevin was kept in ignorance of it.[19]

In his Judgment, Lord Sumption stated that *'section 140A is deliberately framed in wide terms with very little in the way of guidance about the criteria*

---

[18] Mrs Plevin was given documentation that disclosed the existence of commission, but not the amount or the recipients of it

[19] See *Plevin v Paragon Personal Finance Ltd* [2014] UKSC 61 at [18]

for its application... it is not possible to state a precise or universal test for its application, which must depend on the court's judgment of all the relevant facts'.[20]

Plevin also acknowledged that *"Section 140A was undoubtedly intended to introduce a broad definition of unfairness, in place of the narrowly framed provisions which had previously governed extortionate credit bargains"*[21] and that *"...the standard of fairness in a debtor-creditor relationship is a matter for the court, on which it must make its own assessment... An altogether wider range of considerations may be relevant... They include the characteristics of the borrower, her sophistication or vulnerability, the facts which she could reasonably be expected to know or assume, the range of choices available to her, and the degree to which the creditor was or should have been aware of these matters".*[22]

The court is therefore arguably empowered with unfettered discretion to determine, on a case-by-case basis, the matters it considers relevant to the issue of unfairness, as well as to the remedies it considers appropriate where unfairness is found. It must not be forgotten, however, that it is the relationship between the parties that must be determined to be unfair—not merely the terms of the agreement itself.

Given that the court will have regard to 'all matters' it considers relevant, a finding of unfairness in one claim on a set of specific facts may not necessarily give rise to unfairness being found in another. Even in cases where the same unfair terms or practices are alleged, the circumstances of a case may be such that unfairness can be found for one claimant and denied for the next. Further, a determination as to the existence of unfairness under section 140A may also be made in relation to a relationship notwithstanding that the relationship may have ended.

---

20 See *Plevin* at [10]

21 See *Plevin* at [29]

22 See *Plevin* at [17]

A claimant's right to a remedy in cases where an unfair relationship exists is not automatic; the court may award compensation to one claimant and decline to do so for another. This divergence in outcomes is frequently observed in claims involving undisclosed commissions relating to the sale of PPI, where the pleadings submitted on behalf of borrowers are often materially identical. Under cross-examination it may be revealed that a particular claimant actively wanted to purchase the insurance policy, or may have even made a claim under it. In such cases, while a finding of unfairness may be relatively straightforward, the court may nonetheless decline to grant any remedy, having regard to the individual circumstances.

Despite the assessment of fairness being fundamentally fact sensitive, there are a number of principles that arise from the case of *Plevin* and cases that have followed, summarised below.

Categories of Unfairness

A claim of alleged unfairness must arise from one of the categories expressly set out at section 140A(1), sub-paragraphs (a) to (c),[23] being any of the terms of the agreement or of any related agreement, the way in which the creditor has exercised or enforced any of their rights under the agreement or any related agreement, and any other thing done (or not done) by, or on behalf of, the creditor (either before the making of the agreement or any related agreement).

The Relationship Itself Must be Unfair

It is the relationship between the lender and the borrower that must be found to be unfair. In cases where the terms of the agreement are not themselves inherently unfair, the court may nonetheless find the

23 See *Plevin* at [10]

relationship to be unfair and *"this will often be because the relationship is so one-sided as substantially to limit the debtor's ability to choose"*.[24]

Matters Relating to the Creditor are Relevant

Section 140A(2) expressly recognises that both matters relating to the creditor and the debtor may be relevant to the assessment of unfairness. Aspects of the agreement that operate harshly against a borrower may be required to protect what the court regards as a legitimate interest of the creditor, and for that reason may not be regarded as unfair.[25]

Inequality in the Relationship is Not Enough by Itself

Plevin recognised that *"The great majority of relationships between commercial lenders and private borrowers are probably characterised by large differences of financial knowledge and expertise. It is an inherently unequal relationship. But it cannot have been Parliament's intention that the generality of such relationships should be liable to be reopened for that reason alone"*. Unfairness does not, therefore, automatically arise as a result of the natural inequality that arises in the relationship between lender and borrower.

[24] See *Plevin* at [10]

[25] See *Plevin* at [10]

Unfairness from an Extreme Inequality of Knowledge and Understanding

The Supreme Court described a sufficiently extreme inequality of knowledge and understanding as "*a classic source of unfairness in any relationship between a creditor and a non-commercial debtor*".[26]

Unfairness from an Inequality of Financial Expertise

Plevin recognised that beyond a point, *"inequality of financial expertise as between the debtor and the creditor is capable of making their relationship unfair. The provision to a financially unsophisticated debtor of bad advice or no advice about the suitability of a relatively complex product like PPI will commonly result in a one-sided relationship substantially limiting the debtor's ability to choose."*.[27]

The Analysis of Unfairness is Not Affected by Time

In the Supreme Court case of *Smith v Royal Bank of Scotland plc* [2023] UKSC 34, it was stated that:

> *"The court must consider the whole history of the relationship – going back not only to the making of the credit agreement but to any relevant act or omission of the creditor before the making of that agreement or any related agreement. This is so without any limit on how long ago the credit agreement or any related agreement was made. The matters to which the court is obliged to have regard under subsection (2) because it thinks them relevant are likewise not limited in time."*[28]

---

26 See *Plevin* at [18]

27 See *Plevin* at [25]

28 See *Smith* at [23]

Compliance with Regulatory Requirements

The Judgment in *Plevin* overturned *Harrison v Black Horse Ltd* [2012] Lloyd's Rep IR 521 which, until *Plevin* was decided, had been the leading case on the relationship between s.140A CCA and the Insurance Conduct of Business rules ('the ICOB rules').

The ICOB rules, which themselves resulted from a considered policy of the Financial Services Authority,[29] did not require an insurance intermediary to volunteer the amount or the existence of commission it would receive in relation to a transaction.

In *Harrison*, commission retained by the lender was 87% of the value of the premium. Despite describing the value of the premium as *"quite startling"*, the court declined to find that an unfair relationship existed owing to the absence of any breach of the ICOB rules either in charging the commission or failing to disclose it.

The Supreme Court held that *Harrison* had been wrongly decided. It was stated at [17]:

> *'The view which a court takes of the fairness or unfairness of a debtor-creditor relationship may legitimately be influenced by the standard of commercial conduct reasonably to be expected of the creditor. The ICOB rules are some evidence of what that standard is. But they cannot be determinative of the question posed by section 140A, because they are doing different things. The fundamental difference is that the ICOB rules impose obligations on insurers Page 9 and insurance intermediaries. Section 140A, by comparison, does not impose any obligation and is not concerned with the question whether the creditor or anyone else is in breach of a duty. It is concerned with the question whether the creditor's relationship with the debtor was unfair. It may*

[29] The FSA was replaced by the FCA on 1 April 2013

be unfair for a variety of reasons, which do not have to involve a breach of duty.'

Resultingly, whilst a proven breach of regulatory requirements is likely to give rise to unfairness, compliance with regulations may not be enough to discharge the burden of proving that an unfair relationship has not arisen.

Following *Plevin*, a helpful summary of the matters that Hamblen J (as he then was) considered were relevant to deciding whether there was an unfair relationship by reference to each of the three categories listed in paragraphs (a) – (c) of Section140 (1) was given in *Deutsche Bank (Suisse) SA v Khan* [2013] EWHC 482, at [346]:

"(1) In relation to the fairness of the terms themselves:

a. whether the term is commonplace and/or in the nature of the product in question;

b. whether there are sound commercial reasons for the term;

c. whether it represents a legitimate and proportionate attempt by the creditor to protect its position;

d. to the extent that a term is solely for the benefit of the lender, whether it exists to protect him from a risk which the debtor does not face;

e. the scale of the lending and whether it was commercial or quasi-commercial in nature (a court is likely to be slower to find unfairness in high value lending arrangements between commercial parties than in credit agreements affecting consumers); an

f. the strength (or otherwise) of the debtors bargaining position;

g. whether the terms have been individually negotiated or are pro forma terms and, if so, whether they have been presented on a "take it or leave it" basis;

(2) In relation to the creditor's conduct before and at the time of formation:

a. whether the creditor applied any pressure on the borrowers to execute the agreement (if an agreement has been entered into with a sense of urgency it will be relevant to consider to what extent responsibility for this lay with the debtor, as distinct from the creditor);

b. whether the creditor understood and had reasonable grounds to believe that the borrower had experience of the relevant arrangements and had available to him the advice of solicitors;

c. whether the creditor had any reason to think that the debtor had not read or understood the terms; and

d. whether the debtor demurred at the time of formation over the terms he now suggests are unfair (this point has particular force if he did complain over other terms.

(3) In relation to the creditor's conduct following formation and leading up to enforcement:

a. whether any demand was prompted by an "improper motive" or was the consequence of an "arbitrary decision";

b. whether the creditor has shown patience and, before leaping to enforcement, has taken steps in the hope of reaching some form of accommodation (for example by attending meetings, engaging in correspondence and/or inviting proposals); and

c. whether the debtor has resisted attempts at accommodation by raising unfounded claims against the creditor."

Summary

The matters the court may consider under the unfair relationship provisions are broad, varied, and arguably unfettered. Because unfairness is highly fact-sensitive, it is not possible to provide definitive examples of what constitutes unfairness and what does not. There is also no guarantee of a remedy even where unfairness is found.

Practitioners should consider the principles arising in *Plevin* and the authorities that have followed when evaluating the merits of an unfair relationship case. A thorough review of reported cases—both where unfairness has been found and where it has been rejected—is essential to inform any evaluation.

CHAPTER EIGHT

EXAMPLES OF UNFAIRNESS – A SUMMARY

There is no limit to what a borrower may allege as giving rise to unfairness in any particular case. As such, guidance on how the courts approach claims of an unfair relationship must be drawn from the analysis of reported decisions.

Outside of PPI-related litigation and some motor finance cases, allegations of unfairness are rarely made by way of a standalone claim. More commonly, allegations are made defensively in response to a creditor seeking enforcement of an agreement, or appear as a residual 'catch all' complaint appended to broader claims based on other causes of action.

While by no means exhaustive, this chapter outlines the most frequently encountered allegations of unfairness. Key case law is discussed in more detail later in this book.

Interest Rates

Rates of interest are often challenged as being unfair, particularly in business lending where agreements often stipulate elevated, non-competitive rates. Business/commercial lenders have enjoyed some success in defeating unfair relationship claims where very high interest rates are justifiable in the circumstances.

Allegations of unfair rates of interest are far less prevalent in relation to personal loans or credit cards issued by mainstream high street lenders. Interest charged on such agreements tend to be reasonable and in line with prevailing market rates.

There is no definitive rate of interest that would automatically be considered unfair, nor is there a rate which would certainly be fair. The court would assess such claims contextually, weighing the interest rate against all other relevant factors in the credit relationship.

Undisclosed or Secret Commissions

Failure to disclose commissions paid by a lender is a classic example of when unfairness may arise, following the principle firmly established by the Supreme Court in *Plevin v Paragon Personal Finance Ltd* [2014] UKSC 61. Since that decision, the courts have regularly found unfairness arising in circumstances where customers are not told that commissions are being paid or retained in relation to their finance agreements.

More recently, this issue has gained renewed prominence in the well-publicised motor finance cases where car dealerships have been paid undisclosed commissions from finance providers. Factually, the dealership who is in the business of selling vehicles would introduce its customers to specific lenders for the purposes of arranging vehicle finance. Throughout the transaction, the customer would be unaware that the finance company had paid a commission to the dealership. In some cases, there would be no disclosure of the commission payment at all (secret commissions), and in others there would have been partial disclosure relating to the existence of the commission payment, but no disclosure as to the amount of the commission (half-secret or partially disclosed). The decision of the Supreme Court is awaited in relation to many aspects of motor finance cases, but it is unlikely to significantly alter the case-by-case approach adopted by the courts in assessing unfairness under section 140A of the CCA 1974.

Size of Commission Payments

In some cases, unfairness will arise as a result of the *size* of the commission being paid rather than as to its existence. In *Plevin*, it was decided that the claimant should be taken to be aware that some commission would have been payable, but in relation to its size, the court recognised that there was a point where commissions became so large in comparison to the size of the PPI premium that potential unfairness inevitably arose. The court declined to define a specific 'tipping point', but the FCA considered it to be 50%.[30]

Regulatory or Statutory Breaches

Unfairness may also arise from a failure to comply with applicable statutory or regulatory obligations. Allegations of non-compliance with the CCA 1974 itself are sometimes relied upon as factors giving rise to unfairness, but in one such case, being *Carey v HSBC Bank Plc* [2009] EWHC 3417 (QB), no unfairness was found arising from the bank's failure to respond appropriately to a request for information under sections 77 or 78 of the CCA 1974.

Borrower's Circumstances

The borrower's individual circumstances are highly relevant in an assessment of unfairness. A vulnerable or financially unsophisticated borrower is likely to be treated differently to an astute business person.

Lending that is unaffordable to the borrower may be considered unfair, but in cases where borrowers have made false declarations at to their credit worthiness, unfairness is less likely to arise.

30 Following the FCA's post-*Plevin* investigation

Business lending where the creditor faces an elevated risk factor is likely to result in onerous contractual terms or the imposition of expensive fees which are often deemed fair. Independent legal advice taken by the borrower prior to entering the agreement will also weigh against a finding of unfairness.

Conduct and Enforcement

Issues of conduct from before or during the period of the credit agreement may give rise to unfairness. False advertising, aggressive marketing, questionable pre-contract business practices and material omissions may all be scrutinised in the unfairness assessment. High pressure sales tactics, and the sale of products unsuitable for borrowers would also be highly relevant.

Frequent borrower complaints include promises made by lenders that are reneged on, the commencement of enforcement action prematurely thus depriving a borrower of sufficient opportunity to comply with a demand, and delaying in enforcement which in turn results in expensive charges and high interest rates being applied to the agreement.

Borrowers frequently also complain about the appointment of LPA Receivers. Whilst the creditor will appoint the receivers following a default in the repayment terms of the agreement, the receivers usually act on behalf of the borrower and will owe duties to them. If the appointment was premature, unfairness may well arise.

Factors in Favour of Creditors

There are a number of considerations that lenders may advance which weigh in their favour when responding to allegations of unfairness. In some cases, lenders can also take a proactive approach by identifying and remedying potential unfairness before or during the course of the credit relationship. The paragraphs that follow set out examples of conduct that may assist lenders in defending such claims.

Evidence of Fair Dealings

Given that the court may consider the whole history of the credit relationship, and that regard is to be had to any matter that it thinks relevant, the complaints of the borrower are not to be considered in isolation and must be evaluated alongside evidence of fair treatment. Creditors may be able to evidence instances of fairness that benefitted the borrower to counterbalance the unfairness allegations.

Factors that may undermine allegations of unfairness include instances where lenders have demonstrated cooperation with borrowers during periods of financial hardship—for example, by granting payment holidays or freezing interest. Further, where lenders have crystallised outstanding debt balances and waived the right to further interest accrual, such conduct will weigh against a finding of unfairness. In PPI-related claims, it will also be highly relevant if the borrower has previously made a successful claim under the policy, as this may diminish the argument for full redress to be ordered.

Delay

A borrower who delays in commencing an unfair relationships claim is now a matter of significance to the assessment of unfairness. In *Smith and another v Royal Bank of Scotland plc* [2023] UKSC 34 it was said that *"If a debtor sits on his or her hands in knowledge of the relevant facts, it would be… inconceivable that a court would think it just to make an order under section 140B of the 1974 Act. This is so, both during the currency of the relationship and in the six years after that relationship has ended."*

In cases where claimant borrowers have engaged the services of claims management companies, delay is a common feature with initial written complaints often being made several years before claims are ultimately issued. In such cases the court should be asked to consider the issue of delay to determine whether in fact unfairness arises. Given that remedies under section 140B are discretionary, courts may decline to grant any relief where delay is unjustified, regardless of the underlying merits of the claim, and even if the claim is itself not time barred.[31]

Remedying Unfairness Voluntarily

An unfair relationship can be made fair by the subsequent actions of the creditor. In the Court of Appeal Judgment in *Smith*[32] at [59] it was acknowledged that a relationship may not always remain the same and that *"the fact that a relationship was unfair in the past does not mean that things cannot change"*.[33] On appeal, the Supreme Court agreed and described those observations as "indisputable".[34] Lenders should therefore be alert to the options available in the event of customer complaints, and can proactively take steps to reverse the effect of unfairness if it so chooses.

Summary

In determining whether a credit relationship is unfair, the court can consider the matters set out at section 140A(1), and is required to have regard to all matters it considers relevant (140A(2). Creditors are entitled to present evidence of matters that demonstrate fairness within the credit

---

31 See *Smith and another v Royal Bank of Scotland plc* [2023] UKSC 34 at [59]

32 [2021] EWCA Civ 1832

33 See *Smith and another v Royal Bank of Scotland plc* [2021] EWCA Civ 1832 at [65]

34 *Smith and another v Royal Bank of Scotland plc* [2023] UKSC 34 at [63]

relationship notwithstanding that those matters are not directly related to the complaint.

Delay is a relevant factor and may prove fatal to a claim that is otherwise valid.

Finally, creditors can cure unfairness at any point during or after the end of the credit relationship. Such steps may ultimately preclude the borrower from obtaining relief under section 140B.

CHAPTER NINE

UNFAIRNESS IN PPI CLAIMS

In the early years of consumer credit litigation, claims based on the unfair relationship provisions were relatively uncommon. This changed dramatically following the Supreme Court's landmark decision in *Plevin v Paragon Personal Finance Ltd* [2014] UKSC 61.

The *Plevin* judgment had an immediate and profound impact on consumer credit litigation, significantly increasing both the volume and scope of claims alleging unfairness. In the aftermath, there was a surge in cases brought before the courts—most of which centred on the sale of payment protection insurance ('PPI').

PPI History

PPI policies had been sold to borrowers alongside mortgages, loans and credit cards since the 1990s. These policies were marketed on the basis that they would cover monthly repayments under credit or mortgage agreements if the customer became unemployed due to redundancy or was unable to work due to illness.

By 2004, major newspapers had begun reporting concerns about the sale of PPI policies by high street banks owing to the fact that such sales were highly profitable, and little of that profit was being returned for the benefit of their customers.

The Financial Services Authority[35] ('FSA') took over regulation of the insurance industry in 2005, and the reported issues around the sale of PPI were highlighted as a priority task to be addressed. By the end of 2005 the FSA had written to the Banks setting out their concerns.

Allegations of aggressive and inappropriate sales tactics soon followed, with the Citizens Advice Bureau adding further pressure after conducting its own investigation into PPI sales practices.

The early complaints fell into three general categories:

a) The PPI policies were expensive. In relation to loan or mortgage agreements, the entire cost of the PPI could be added upfront to the loan amount, to then be paid off over the term of the loan (such models were known as 'single premium' PPI policies) with interest. A successful sale of PPI could add 20% or more onto the overall cost of the credit agreement. In relation to credit cards, PPI would usually be charged each month as a percentage of the outstanding balance on the customer's statement. If the customer made only the minimum required monthly payments, compound interest would be charged on the entire outstanding balance which included the PPI premium.

b) The PPI policies were mis-sold. This category covered a number of scenarios including financially unsophisticated customers being given no choice as to whether they bought PPI, PPI being represented as a compulsory product when in fact it was optional, and being advised to take out PPI when the policies were of little or no benefit to customers. It was routinely the case that customers who had purchased PPI would later discover that their policies did not, or would not have benefitted them had they needed to make a claim. Some customers already benefitted from

35 The Financial Services Authority became the Financial Conduct Authority in 2013

generous sickness payments from their employers, and in other cases claims were rejected by the insurer owing to the policy holder being self-employed. Frequently, the policies sold required self-employed people to de-register their self-employment status in order to be brought within the scope of the policy.

c) The policies were ineffective or inefficient. Successful payouts on policies were considered rare, and claims were not being dealt with promptly resulting in dire financial issues having already arisen for customers by the time the policy paid out.

From 2005, a number of high-profile fines were issued by the FSA regarding various findings of PPI mis-selling. One of the earliest fines to be imposed was against Regency Mortgage Corporation. The FSA found that PPI policies had been sold to mortgage customers purchasing properties under the 'Right To Buy' scheme in circumstances where such customers would not have been eligible to make a claim. A penalty of £56,000.00 was imposed.

Further investigations followed and the financial penalties increased. A fine of £860,000.00 was imposed upon Liverpool Victoria Banking Services. At the time, this was the second largest fine ever imposed by the FSA, yet it would have been higher had the Bank not agreed to pay compensation to its customers. The FSA investigation uncovered that between 2005 and 2007 Liverpool Victoria's call centres would take enquiries for unsecured loans and would generate quotations that would unilaterally include a single premium PPI. In the event that the charge was questioned, customers were pressured into agreeing to it. Around 14,500 policies were sold during a 2.5-year period. Liverpool Victoria subsequently refunded all interest paid in relation to the PPI premiums without customers having to complain.

Alliance & Leicester was fined £7 million on account of its staff having been trained to put pressure on customers who questioned the inclusion of PPI in their loan quotations, and HFC Bank was fined £1.1m for poor PPI sales practices.

In 2007, The Office for Fair Trading became involved and the sale of PPI policies was referred to the Competition Commission.

In 2008, the reported 'scandal' escalated with Which? reporting that one in three customers who had purchased PPI had been sold a worthless product.

In 2009 the FSA imposed a ban on the sale of single premium PPI policies which had been added to loans at inception, thus attracting high rates of interest over a long period of time.

By 2011 the high street banks announced that they would be setting aside billions of pounds to deal with compensation claims from dissatisfied customers. Despite the stance taken, many banks were routinely rejecting compensation claims. Customers had better results when complaints were referred to the Financial Ombudsman Service. Over time, the financial implications of the PPI scandal were significant for lenders.

The FSA introduced a new regime for PPI sales which took effect retrospectively. The decision was challenged by the British Banking Association by way of Judicial Review, but they were defeated in the High Court. As a result, the banks were forced to re-open mis-selling claims and also investigate and identify any customers entitled to compensation.

Large scale litigation followed despite internal complaints procedures being free for use by customers. For those cases that were litigated, decisions from the court varied widely. Successful claims usually related to PPI policies that could be readily established as unsuitable for a particular claimant, for example for the reason of being self-employed.

Unfairness Following *Plevin*

The pivotal finding in *Plevin* that triggered the surge in PPI litigation was set out by Lord Sumption at [18]:

> *"I turn therefore to the question whether the non-disclosure of the commissions payable out of Mrs Plevin's PPI premium made her relationship with Paragon unfair. In my opinion, it did. A sufficiently extreme inequality of knowledge and understanding is a classic source of unfairness in any relationship between a creditor and a non-commercial debtor. It is a question of degree. Mrs Plevin must be taken to have known that some commission would be payable to intermediaries out of the premium before it reached the insurer. The fact was stated in the FISA borrowers' guide and, given that she was not paying LLP for their services, there was no other way that they could have been remunerated. But at some point commissions may become so large that the relationship cannot be regarded as fair if the customer is kept in ignorance. At what point is difficult to say, but wherever the tipping point may lie the commissions paid in this case are a long way beyond it. Mrs Plevin's evidence, as recorded by the Recorder, was that if she had known that 71.8% of the premium would be paid out in commissions, she would have "certainly questioned this." I do not find that evidence surprising. The information was of critical relevance. Of course, had she shopped around, she would not necessarily have got better terms. As the Competition Commission's report suggests, this was not a competitive market. But Mrs Plevin did not have to take PPI at all. Any reasonable person in her position who was told that more than two thirds of the premium was going to intermediaries, would be bound to question whether the insurance represented value for money, and whether it was a sensible transaction to enter into. The fact that she was left in ignorance in my opinion made the relationship unfair."*

It is a common misconception that the *Plevin* judgment automatically establishes unfairness in similar cases and guarantees a remedy in favour of the customer. In reality, claimants cannot rely solely on the non-disclosure of substantial commission to prove that a credit relationship was unfair. Each case must be assessed on its own merits, and the burden remains on the claimant to establish the necessary facts. Claimants who elect not to attend court and provide oral evidence in support of their claims do so at considerable risk; in such circumstances, claims may be dismissed for want of evidence.

One example of a case where the court did not find unfairness despite the existence of a substantial undisclosed commission was *Hodell and Others v Clydesdale Bank plc* [2018] EWHC 1009 (QB). In that case the court took into account the fact that the claimant was a non-vulnerable, sophisticated businessperson, such facts weighing against any finding of unfairness.

FCA guidance

Another recurring feature of PPI litigation is the argument that any unfairness that existed as a result of excessive commission payments has been remedied following the payment of subsequent compensation by the lender.

Following the decision in *Plevin*, the FCA consulted on the widespread problem of non-disclosure of PPI commissions and, in May 2017, issued a policy statement that led to the implementation of detailed guidance in Appendix 3 to the FCA's Dispute Resolution: Complaints sourcebook (DISP).[36]

Under this guidance, where a complaint involves undisclosed commission exceeding 50% of the total PPI premium, the lender is required to presume that such non-disclosure gave rise to an unfair relationship under section 140A of the CCA 1974.[37] Where the lender determined that the relationship was indeed unfair, it was required to

[36] Commonly referred to as 'Disp App 3'

[37] The presumption was rebuttable under DISP App 3.3A.5

provide redress by refunding the portion of commission exceeding 50%, along with any interest charged on that amount under the credit agreement, and compensatory interest at a rate of 8% per annum.

In claims where claimants have received compensation under the FCA redress scheme, lenders can validly argue that any unfairness that existed has been cured, the agreement is no longer unfair and/or that no further redress should be awarded to the claimant. This argument has been met with mixed success in the courts. Its effectiveness varies on a case-by-case basis, and there is no consistent judicial approach that provides a reliable indicator of the likely outcome.

Relief

Whilst the broad range of powers that the court holds under section 140B is discussed in more detail in chapter 11, it is worth considering here the likely outcomes in PPI cases where a declaration of unfairness is made.

In the first instance decision of *Doran v Paragon Personal Finance* [2018 ECC 32], HHJ Pearce approached the exercise of discretion in this way [72] – [74]:

> *72. In so far as the court approaches the issue of remedy from the view point of seeking to compensate the claimants for financial loss, there is a tension between awarding the sum claimed by the claimants (which arguably over-compensates them because it fails to give credit for the peace of mind that the PPI policy brought) and the defendant's approach (which arguably undercompensates the claimants because it requires them to give credit for the cost of a product which they would not have in fact incurred but for the unfairness).*
>
> *73. The Court in this situation might be tempted to reach some kind of halfway house to give a notional figure for the peace of mind that the PPI policy provided. However, it is not at all obvious to me how I could properly put a value on such peace of mind.*

> *74. It is relevant to bear in mind that this is a remedy which arises because of unfairness in a relationship between stronger and weaker bargaining parties. Whilst there can be no suggestion that the remedy is intended to be punitive, there is in my judgment good reason to err in favour of the party who has been treated unfairly.*

Remedies generally fall into two categories:

- A refund of the full value of the commission with associated contractual interest and fees, commonly referred to as the *'Platts method'*;[38]

- A refund of all sums paid in relation to the PPI policy, together with associated interest and fees charged.

Credit is usually given for any sums paid under the FCA redress scheme.

In addition to the primary remedy, discretionary interest is additionally usually awarded. It should be noted that interest cannot be claimed pursuant to Section 69 of the County Courts Act 1984, as an unfair relationship claim it is not a claim for debt or damages. In awarding discretionary interest, the court may consider any issues of delay on the part of the claimant, and will usually award between 2% and 8% per annum.

Summary

The *Plevin* decision in 2014 led to a huge rise in cases concerning unfair treatment related to the sale of PPI. Claims that are now litigated are usually brought solely on the basis that an unfair relationship arose owing to the payment of large undisclosed commissions.

---

38 This method was used in the *Plevin* case after it had been remitted back to the lower court for determination of remedy.

Not every case with hidden commission is automatically unfair — unfairness is determined in the context of the credit relationship as a whole.

After *Plevin*, the FCA set rules and guidance requiring redress to be paid to complainants if more than half of the PPI premium was undisclosed commission. Unfairness was to be presumed in such cases.

Courts sometimes agree that the redress already paid under the FCA scheme cures unfairness, but sometimes they do not. Alternative remedies include ordering the return of all of the commission and associated interest to claimants (known as the 'Platts method'), and refunding the entirety of all sums paid by customers in relation to the PPI. In either case, compensatory interest is almost always ordered in addition.

CHAPTER TEN

UNFAIRNESS IN MOTOR FINANCE CLAIMS

Motor finance litigation has emerged as a rapidly expanding area of consumer claims and, in recent months, has appeared poised to surpass PPI claims in terms of the volume expected to proceed through the courts.

The development of such cases began in July 2020 following a policy statement being issued by the FCA regarding certain commission models which incentivised car dealers and motor finance brokers to maximise the cost of credit agreements for customers. This commission model[39] which was ultimately banned by the FCA gave autonomy to the dealer/broker to increase (or decrease) the rate of interest charged under an agreement with higher interest rates leading to higher rates of commission being paid to the dealer/broker. Such models were defined broadly by the FCA:

> *"...to make clear that it includes where any commission, fee or other financial consideration is payable directly or indirectly in connection with the regulated credit agreement, and where this is wholly or partly affected by the interest rate (or other item within the total charge for credit) set or negotiated by the broker".*[40]

A number of causes of action are said to arise from such commission arrangements, including regulatory breaches, bribery as a result of payment of a secret commission, and unfair relationship.

---

39 Known by the FCA as 'Discretionary Commission Arrangement'

40 PS20/8

Similarly to what occurred with PPI cases, claims management companies have embarked on highly publicised marketing campaigns to attract consumers who may have been unaware of the commissions being paid in relation to the purchase of their motor vehicle.

In January 2024, the FCA announced that it was to review firms' historical motor finance discretionary commission models and sales owing to the number of complaints being made to lenders which involved the payment of commissions before the ban took effect.

Early first instance decisions in litigated motor finance claims produced highly inconsistent outcomes. Where claimants succeeded on a primary cause of action—such as breach of duty—findings of unfairness under the CCA 1974 often followed. Conversely, where the primary claim failed, courts typically rejected all pleaded grounds, including unfair relationship allegations. As a result, legal practitioners widely sought authoritative guidance in the form of a binding appellate decision. That guidance came firstly from the Court of Appeal in *Johnson v FirstRand Bank Ltd (London Branch) (t/a MotoNovo Finance)* [2024] EWCA Civ 1282.

Johnson concerned three conjoined appeals (*Johnson v FirstRand Bank Ltd, Wrench v FirstRand Bank Ltd* and *Hopcraft v Close Brothers Ltd*) all based on similar facts. The claimants were financially unsophisticated individuals who purchased a second-hand car from a dealership. The dealerships in each case assisted the customer in obtaining finance to fund the purchase of the motor vehicle.

The claimants entered into motor finance agreements with finance providers, and the agreements were said to have been 'arranged' by the respective car dealerships. In each case, the lender paid a commission to the dealership for introducing the customer. The structure of these commissions mirrored the type later prohibited by the FCA—specifically, a discretionary or variable commission model under which the dealer's remuneration increased in proportion to the interest rate charged to the borrower. There was a factual difference between the three cases regarding evidence of disclosures made to the customer regarding the payment of commission.

In the Johnson appeal it was contended that *"...the relationship between him and FirstRand was unfair, because the relationship resulted in a hire purchase agreement and associated personal loan agreement being concluded when the commission agreement between FirstRand and the Trade Centre Wales had not been disclosed in a way which actually brought it to his attention, and explained its true significance. He contended that this was "a thing....not done...on behalf of [the lender]" by the broker which gave rise to an unfair relationship."*[41]

The appeals were allowed in their entirety. While the majority of the Court of Appeal's judgment focuses on the substantive issues of agency, the duties owed by the dealerships, and allegations of bribery, the court also made a significant finding of unfairness under section 140A of the CCA 1974 in relation to Mr Johnson's case. Notably, the court held that there had been no effective disclosure of commission, notwithstanding that the lender had included a reference to the existence of commission payments within its standard terms and conditions. The court concluded that the disclosure was insufficient, as it had not been specifically brought to Mr Johnson's attention and he had not read the relevant documentation. The following points were made:

> *"So far as the statutory claim is concerned, the mere fact that there has been no disclosure of the commission, or only partial disclosure, will not necessarily suffice to make the relationship between lender and consumer "unfair" for the purposes of the 1974 Act. However on its specific facts, Mr Johnson's claim under the 1974 Act succeeds."*[42]

> *"We are quite satisfied that the relationship between the lender and Mr Johnson arising out of the agreement was unfair to Mr Johnson because*

41 See *Johnson* at [144]

42 See *Johnson at* [20]

> *of things done (or not done) by, or on behalf of, the lender, FirstRand (either before or after the making of the agreement or any related agreement). Fairness in this context is a matter of degree, and the fact that the commission to the broker was 25% of the sum advanced is a key fact, as is the fact that the sum borrowed and paid to the dealer was much more than the car was worth. The fact that this very bad bargain arose from a relationship between the broker and the lender which was falsified by the broker, and not disclosed by the lender, is also critical."*[43]

> *"A relationship will not necessarily be unfair for the purposes of the 1974 Act simply because a broker receives a commission from the lender and the borrower is not actually aware of that fact. The court is required to consider all the facts and to weigh their importance. If the commission is very high in relation to the sum borrowed that may, in itself, be enough to make the relationship unfair where nothing, or nothing of substance, has been done to disclose the relationship between the lender and the broker. It is not necessary to develop this analysis further for the purposes of the appeal in Johnson because the commission was very high in that case, and the true nature of the relationship between the lender and the broker was not disclosed by the lender and actively concealed by the broker (acting as agent for the lender by virtue of section 56 of the 1974 Act). It is a very clear case."*[44]

Johnson is therefore yet another case where the court has recognised that very high rates of commission will be relevant to the assessment of fairness. Unfairness arising from the non-disclosure of commission and/or the pre-existing relationship between the lender and the dealer/broker is perhaps unsurprising given the decision in *Plevin*, but the position regarding the steps a lender should take to make such disclosures remains unclear.

---

43 See *Johnson* at [169]

44 See *Johnson* at [170]

Appeal to the Supreme Court

The Supreme Court heard the lenders' conjoined appeal over 3 days at the start of April 2024. The decision[45] is awaited.

Since the Court of Appeal decision, the FCA published a statement on its website confirming its ongoing review of the past use of motor finance discretionary commission arrangements and confirming it was *"seeking to understand if firms failed to comply with requirements relating to DCAs and if consumers lost out as a result."*

A PPI style redress scheme appears to be likely, with the FCA *"...confirming that if, taking into account the Supreme Court's decision, we conclude motor finance customers have lost out from widespread failings by firms, then it's likely we will consult on an industry-wide redress scheme."*

Although the FCA had initially indicated that an update would be provided in May 2025, this timeline has since been delayed. The FCA has now confirmed that a decision as to whether to propose a formal redress scheme will be made within six weeks of the Supreme Court's expected judgment.

Summary

The volume of motor finance claims being brought before the courts has increased significantly, driven in large part by extensive media coverage highlighting potential claims arising from undisclosed commission payments in connection with vehicle purchases. Allegations of unfair relationships have featured prominently in the majority of these claims.

In *Johnson v FirstRand Bank Ltd*, the Court of Appeal held that an unfair relationship did arise, citing in particular the lender's failure to disclose the commission in any meaningful way and the disproportionately high

45 Case ID UKSC/2024/0158

level of that commission. However, the mere existence of an undisclosed commission does not, in and of itself, give rise to automatic unfairness under section 140A of the CCA 1974.The Supreme Court has now heard the conjoined appeals launched by the lenders. The decision is awaited.

CHAPTER ELEVEN

REMEDIES

Once the court has made a declaration of an unfair relationship under section 140A of the CCA 1974, it must then proceed to the second stage and determine, in the exercise of its discretion, whether it is appropriate to grant a remedy under section 140B.

The remedies available to the court are expressly set out in section 140B(1). The court may grant one or more of the following:

a) An order requiring the creditor, or any associate or former associate of his, to repay (in whole or in part) any sum paid by the debtor or by a surety by virtue of the agreement or any related agreement (whether paid to the creditor, the associate or the former associate or to any other person);

b) An order requiring the creditor, or any associate or former associate of his, to do or not to do (or to cease doing) anything specified in the order in connection with the agreement or any related agreement;

c) An order to reduce or discharge any sum payable by the debtor or by a surety by virtue of the agreement or any related agreement;

d) An order to direct the return to a surety of any property provided by him for the purposes of a security;

e) An order to otherwise set aside (in whole or in part) any duty imposed on the debtor or on a surety by virtue of the agreement or any related agreement;

f) An order to alter the terms of the agreement or of any related agreement;

g) An order directing accounts to be taken, or (in Scotland) an accounting to be made, between any persons.

The court has "considerable discretionary latitude" when deciding whether to grant a remedy under section 140B. While the power is discretionary, a finding of unfairness will generally lead to some form of relief being awarded to address the imbalance in the relationship.[46]

In *Smith v Royal Bank of Scotland*,[47] the Supreme Court reaffirmed that "*…the legislation also gives the court, where a determination of unfairness is made, the broadest possible remedial discretion in deciding what order, if any, to make under section 140B. Section 140B gives the court an extensive menu of options from which to select but says nothing at all about how this selection may or should be made. On the face of the legislation the court's discretion is entirely unfettered.*"[48]

However, *Smith* does acknowledge that the court's discretion under section 140B, while broad, is not entirely without limits. The judgment recognises that the general purpose of an order under section 140B is, in principle, "*…to remove the cause(s) of the unfairness which the court has identified, if they are still continuing, and to reverse any damaging financial consequences to the debtor of that unfairness, so that the relationship as a whole can no longer be regarded as unfair.*"[49]

46 See *Kerrigan v Elevate Credit International Ltd (t/a Sunny) (In Administration)* [2020] EWHC 2169 at [216]

47 *Smith v Royal Bank of Scotland* [2023] UKSC 34

48 See *Smith* at [25]

49 See *Smith* at [25]

In the earlier High Court case of *Carney v N M Rothschild & Sons Limited* [2018] EWHC 958 (Comm), having considered a number of previous decisions, HHJ Waksman KC stated:[50]

> *"...the Court has a wide discretion as to any relief to be ordered once the unfair relationship has been found... if the court decides to make an order, then it 'should reflect and be proportionate to the nature and degree of unfairness which the court has found': Patel v Patel [2010] 1 All ER (Comm) 864 at [79]- [80] . It should not give the Claimant a windfall, but should approximate, as closely as possible, the overall position which would have applied had the matters giving rise to the perceived unfairness not taken place: Link Finance Limited v Wilson [2014] CTLC. 145 at [77] ; Chubb & Bruce v Dean [2013] EWHC 1282 (Ch) at [24] ; Nelmes v NRAM Plc [2006] EWCA Civ 491 at [116]."*

Causation

The issue of causation was considered in *Kerrigan v Elevate Credit International Ltd (t/a Sunny) (In Administration)* [2020] EWHC 2169 (Comm). Noting that section 140A(1) did not impose a requirement of causation "*...in the sense that a debtor must show that a breach caused a loss for an award of substantial damages to be made.*",[51] the court affirmed that "*...the focus is on the unfairness of the relationship, and the court's approach to the granting of relief is informed by that, rather than by a demonstration that a particular act caused a particular loss.*"

The judgment in *Kerrigan* acknowledges that the court is not free to "simply do anything," and explained:

---

50 See *Carney* at [101]

51 See *Kerrigan* at [213]

> *"There is a link between (i) the failings of the creditor which lead to the unfairness in the relationship, (ii) the unfairness itself, and (iii) the relief. It is not to be analysed in the sort of linear terms which arise when considering causation proper. The court is to have regard to all the relevant circumstances when determining whether the relationship is unfair, and the same sort of approach applies when considering what relief is required to remedy that unfairness."*[52]

Causation was also addressed by HHJ Waksman KC in his judgment in *Carney* where he suggested that relief under section 140B may not be appropriate if the matters complained of resulted in no material impact on the borrower:

> *"Causation is perhaps less straightforward. In cases of wrong advice and misrepresentation it would be odd if any relief could be considered if they did not have at least some material impact on the debtor when deciding whether or not to enter the agreement. And thus in Plevin, whilst the unfairness was said to be the failure to disclose the commission, there was at least a finding that the debtor would have "certainly questioned this" the size of the commission being of "critical relevance"... But in a case like the one before me, if in fact the debtors would have entered into the agreement in any event, this must surely count against a finding of unfair relationship under s140A."*[53]

Proportionality

If the court decides to award a remedy, then it should reflect and be proportionate to the nature and degree of unfairness which has been identified.[54] The remedy should not provide the claimant a windfall, but should instead aim to restore the parties to the position they would have

52 See *Kerrigan* at [214]

53 See *Carney* at [51]

54 See *Kerrigan* and *Patel v Patel* [2009] EWHC 3264 (QB) at [79 -80]

been in had the unfairness not occurred.[55] The objective is to ensure fairness, not to punish the creditor or overcompensate the debtor.

The court in *Kerrigan* found the decision of HHJ Keyser KC in *Brookman v Welcome Financial Services* to be of particular assistance in relation to the approach to be taken. *Brookman* was argued in the Mercantile Court but judgment was handed down in the county court at Cardiff on 6 November 2015. The case is unreported, but a transcript was provided to the court in *Kerrigan,* and the 'remedy' remarks extracted and restated. The conclusions are set out at paragraph [47] of the *Kerrigan* judgment and can be summarised as follows:

- The court has a discretion, not a duty, to grant a remedy. However, if the court is able by the grant of a remedy to relieve a debtor from unfairness, it is likely that it will seek to do so.

- The court's powers are wide.

- In view of the nature of the determination that grounds the discretion, the purpose of the powers must be to relieve from unfairness, not to compensate the debtor or punish the creditor.

- The unfairness in *Kerrigan* consisted in the claimants assuming liability in respect of PPI agreements with inadequate knowledge to have been able to make properly informed decisions. The consequence of the decisions that they made was that they had and retained liability in respect of the residual premiums and interest in that regard even after the PPI agreements were cancelled.

- There is no good reason for declining to grant a remedy in respect of the unfairness that was found to exist.

---

55 See *Kerrigan* at [214]

- The statutory powers do not require that the remedy be fashioned so as to eliminate all onerous consequences of the transaction entered into in circumstances where the debtor's decision-making was impaired. It does not follow that, because the claimants incurred the liability for PPI in circumstances of unfairness, they must necessarily be relieved of all such liability.

Summary

Claims of unfair relationship involve a 2-stage test. Firstly, the court must decide whether there exists unfairness for the purposes of section 140A. If so, the court should secondly consider whether it is appropriate to order a remedy to correct the unfairness. The decision to order a remedy is in the discretion of the court. Although a finding of unfairness will usually result in a remedy being awarded to a complainant, there is no automatic right to one.

Any award should not be penal or give rise to a windfall for a claimant. While strict causation does not need to be proven, any remedy should aim to address the causes of unfairness identified by the court and, if ongoing, to reverse any resulting financial harm to the debtor—so that the relationship as a whole is no longer to be regarded as unfair.

CHAPTER TWELVE

KEY REPORTED CASES

This chapter reviews many of the key reported cases concerning unfair relationship claims. While some cases are mentioned in other chapters, they are repeated here for ease of reference. Cases are grouped under broad categories, but there is a great degree of overlap as to the matters that were considered in each case. As such, the main allegations of unfairness are noted beneath each case name.

<u>Undisclosed Commissions</u>

Plevin v Paragon Personal Finance Limited **[2014] 1 WLR 4222**

Non-disclosure of commission payments, excessively high commissions

Plevin remains the leading case on unfair relationships. Factually, the allegations of unfairness centred on the non-disclosure of excessive commissions paid by the lender under a credit agreement to the borrower's broker. Whie the findings in *Plevin* caused a huge influx of claims regarding the sale of payment protection insurance, it remains the case that the existence of an undisclosed commission will not, by itself, give rise to any automatic unfairness.

The decision held that Mrs Plevin was to be taken to know that a commission was payable to intermediaries from the premium before it reached the insurer. In finding unfairness, Lord Sumption said at [18]:

> *"I turn therefore to the question whether the non-disclosure of the commissions payable out of Mrs Plevin's PPI premium made her relationship with Paragon unfair. In my opinion, it did. A sufficiently extreme inequality of knowledge and understanding is a classic source*

> *of unfairness in any relationship between a creditor and a non-commercial debtor. It is a question of degree. Mrs Plevin must be taken to have known that some commission would be payable to intermediaries out of the premium before it reached the insurer. The fact was stated in the FISA borrowers' guide and, given that she was not paying LLP for their services, there was no other way that they could have been remunerated. But at some point commissions may become so large that the relationship cannot be regarded as fair if the customer is kept in ignorance."*

It follows that, in Mrs Plevin's case, unfairness arose as a result of the size of the commission rather than its mere existence. Furthermore, the court held that the responsibility of disclosing the amount of the commission rested with the lender. Had the lender informed Mrs Plevin of the amount of commission *'unfairness would have been removed because Mrs Plevin would then have been able to make a properly informed about the value of the PPI policy'*.[56]

Plevin also establishes that a claimant only needs to show that the commission would have been questioned had they been disclosed; it is not necessary for a claimant to provide evidence as to what decision may ultimately have been made.

Nelmes v NRAM Plc [2016] EWCA Civ 491

Secret Commissions

In *Nelmes,* the Court declared that an unfair relationship did exist as a result of the payment of a secret commission to a broker.

Mr Nelmes owned a portfolio of residential properties and engaged the services of a broker to source finance that would allow him to consolidate his debts and obtain further funding. The broker arranged two

[56] See Plevin paragraph 20

commercial loans between Mr Nelmes and Northern Rock PLC (now NRAM Plc). The loans totalled £2.85m, and Mr Nelmes was required to pay an arrangement fee to the broker of 0.75%.

Whilst the loan offers disclosed that the arrangement fees to be paid by Mr Nelmes to Northern Rock were £21,483 in respect of one loan and £8,500 in respect of another, it was not disclosed to Mr Nelmes that Northern Rock Plc in fact paid half of those arrangement fees on to the broker by way of secret commission.

Mr Nelmes brought a claim of unfair relationship against NRAM on the basis of a number of factors, including the terms of the loan offer, NRAM's conduct, and the relationship between NRAM and the broker.

The Court found there to be an unfair relationship, but only on the issue of the undisclosed commission. It was stated at [35]:

> "*The claim against NR*[57] *in the present action is not a claim that it should account for the commission or for rescission of the credit agreement, but that relief should be given because of the unfair nature of the relationship. That claim raises different, and broader, considerations. I am, however, quite satisfied that in this respect the relationship between NR, the creditor, and Mr Nelmes, the debtor, arising out of the loan agreements was unfair on account of the combination of the following: (i) the term of the credit agreement that Mr Nelmes should pay NR an arrangement fee; (ii) the related agreement that NR should pay commission of half that amount to Mr Nelmes' broker; (iii) the payment of that commission; and (iv) the failure of NR to tell Nelmes about the payment. A relationship between lender and borrower which involves such a payment deprives the borrower of the disinterested advice of his broker and is, for that reason, unfair.*"

57 NRAM/Northern Rock

Swift Advances Plc v Scott [2019] NICh 16

Undisclosed Commission, unsuitable PPI product

Swift Advances was a case heard and decided in Northern Ireland. An unfair relationship was found in favour of borrowers who had taken out a loan in the sum of £28,500, which included the sum of £3,500 for a personal protection insurance premium. The court held that the PPI policy had been mis-sold to the borrowers. Although the term of the loan was ten years, the policy only provided protection for five years. It was determined that the policy had been sold primarily in order for the lender to benefit from a large commission payment rather than for the benefit it conferred on the borrowers. By way of remedy, the borrowers were released from any liability in relation to the PPI premium.

Wood v Commercial First Business Ltd (In Liquidation) [2019] EWHC 2205 (Ch)

Undisclosed commission

In *Wood*, the claimant sought to set aside three mortgage agreements on the grounds that her broker had received undisclosed commissions from the lender.

The court found in her favour, holding that the commissions were "fully secret" as Mrs Wood had not been properly informed of them. Although the broker's terms mentioned that commission might be paid, the amounts were not disclosed, and written notice had not been provided. As a result, the court ruled that the mortgage agreements should be rescinded, subject to counter-restitution.

The lender was ordered to repay over £92,000 in undisclosed commission. The decision reinforced the principle that where commission payments are not transparently disclosed, especially in consumer or small business lending contexts, the borrower may be entitled to significant relief. It was further held that the commission payments also deprived the borrower of her broker's disinterested advice, and the relationship between the borrower and the lender was unfair for the purposes of section 140A of the CCA 1974.

Pengelly v Business Mortgage Finance 4 Plc [2020] EWHC 2002 (Ch)

Commission payment

Pengelly was a case where the sole basis for alleging unfairness was payment of a commission received by his broker in relation to a mortgage that he had arranged. No unfairness was found to have arisen.

Mr Pengelly was aware, or was deemed to be aware of the possibility of the payment of commission and had made no enquiries about it. It was held that the lender had provided Mr Pengelly with the mortgage that he wanted at a fair and competitive rate.

There was no evidence that Mr Pengelly would have acted in any other way had he been aware of the commission payment. In those circumstances, the court declined to find that there was anything unfair about the relationship.

The validity of the decision in *Pengelly* may be materially affected by the judgment of the Supreme Court expected in relation to secret commissions in motor finance claims.

Secret Commissions in Motor Finance

Johnson v Firstrand Bank Limited (London Branch) T/A Motonovo Finance [2024] EWCA Civ 1282

Undisclosed commissions, breach of duty, regulatory breaches

Arguably the most pivotal recent consumer case is that of *Johnson v Firstrand Bank.* The case involved the conjoined appeals of *Johnson, Wrench v Firstrand Bank Limited (London Branch) T/A Motonovo Finance*, and *Hopcraft & Hopcraft v Close Brothers Ltd.*

The decision of the Court of Appeal is itself challenged and the decision of the Supreme Court is awaited.

While the three claims primarily focused on the duties owed by credit intermediaries (brokers) acting as car dealers and the alleged breaches of those duties, they also included allegations of unfair relationships under sections 140A–C of the CCA 1974.

The unfairness allegation was that the relationship between the borrower and the lender arising out of the credit agreements was unfair owing to the non-disclosure of the amount of the commission and/or because commission was paid by the lender to the broker in circumstances which rendered the broker in breach of his duties to the customer.

Only the unfair relationship claim in *Johnson* was considered by the Court of Appeal.

Mr Johnson's argument was that an unfair relationship arose from the agreement between him and FirstRand because a hire purchase agreement and associated personal loan agreement were concluded in circumstances where the commission agreement between FirstRand and the broker had not been disclosed '*in a way which actually brought it to his attention, and explained its true significance. He contended that this was "a thing....not done...on behalf of [the lender]" by the broker which gave rise to an unfair relationship.*[58]

Notably, *Johnson* reaffirmed that no automatic unfairness arises from the non-disclosure of commission. It was said at [20]:

> *'So far as the statutory claim is concerned, the mere fact that there has been no disclosure of the commission, or only partial disclosure, will not necessarily suffice to make the relationship between to make the relationship between lender and consumer "unfair" for the purposes of the 1974 Act.'*

FirstRand accepted that the broker was its agent, thus section 140A(1)(c) was engaged.

The Court of Appeal declared an unfair relationship in favour of Mr Johnson. Whilst it was found that the commission had not been disclosed, the matters taken into account when considering the issue of unfairness included proven breaches of the CONC rules,[59] the fact that the commission paid to the broker was 25% of the sum advanced, and the fact that the sum borrowed and paid to the dealer was much more than the car was worth.

The Court described the agreement as a '*very bad bargain*'[60] arising from a relationship between the broker and the lender, which was falsified by the broker, and not disclosed by the lender.

Having found the relationship to be unfair, the court stated that a '*...relationship will not necessarily be unfair for the purposes of the 1974 Act simply because a broker receives a commission from the lender and the*

58 See *Johnson v Firstrand Bank Limited (London Branch) T/A Motonovo Finance* [2024] EWCA Civ 1282 at [144]

59 CONC – Consumer Credit Sourcebook

60 See *Johnson* at [169]

borrower is not actually aware of that fact. The court is required to consider all the facts and to weigh their importance. If the commission is very high in relation to the sum borrowed that may, in itself, be enough to make the relationship unfair where nothing, or nothing of substance, has been done to disclose the relationship between the lender and the broker.'[61]

While submissions on remedy were not heard, the court's view on the appropriate solution was clear: the lender should repay Mr Johnson the £1,650 commission, along with any interest he paid on that amount under the hire purchase and personal loan agreements. Interest on those two elements should also be awarded at an '*appropriate commercial rate from the date of the agreement*'.[62]

Jones v BMW Financial Services (GB) Ltd [2024] WL 01075512

Undisclosed Commission

Jones was a first instance decision following a claim heard in the County Court at Liverpool before His Honour Judge Richard Carter.

Mr Jones had entered into a hire-purchase agreement with the defendant ('BMW') in order to finance the purchase of a car.

The dealership who supplied the car introduced Mr Jones to BMW. The duration of the hire purchase agreement was 47 months, with an interest rate of 5.4% APR. BMW paid the motor dealer a £300 commission.

Within the terms of the hire purchase agreement, it was disclosed by BMW that a commission might be payable, but the amount of that commission was not disclosed.

---

61 See *Johnson* at [170]

62 See *Johnson* at [172]

Mr Jones asserted that he had not read the terms and conditions of the hire purchase agreement in any detail and that he had been unaware of the commission. It was said that Mr Jones was financially unsophisticated, and had been mostly concerned with the affordability of the monthly payments under the hire purchase agreement.

Mr Jones said that had he known of the commission he would have considered his options to see whether he could have obtained a better rate of interest elsewhere.

Whilst the claim brought by Mr Jones focussed heavily on breach of duty by the dealership, an unfair relationship claim was also made based upon the same facts; that BMW had paid a half secret commission to the dealership.

In finding that BMW had paid the dealership a hidden (half secret) commission, and that such a payment gave rise to an unfair relationship, the court acknowledged the overlap between remedies to correct unfairness, and equitable compensation which Mr Jones was entitled to under his successful breach of duty claim. The Court stated at [75 – 76]:

> *"75. Bearing in mind my conclusions on the half-secret commission claim above there is a clear overlap between the remedy of equitable compensation and the unfairness under s 140A and the remedies available under s 140B. The failure of the Defendant to comply with the OFT guidance is another factor which the Court can take into account when determining unfairness.*
>
> *76. However, that unfairness extends only to the non-disclosure of the payment of the commission to the dealer and no further. The appropriate remedy for such unfairness would be the same remedy I have already found appropriate for the breach of fiduciary duty."*

The court ordered a return of the commission together with interest at the contractual rate under the agreement. This was considered by the court to be the appropriate remedy under equitable compensation principles, and also to correct the unfairness arising from the agreement.

It is notable that interest at the contractual rate was ordered, as this is a commonly sought remedy in cases involving secret commissions. On a commission payment of only £300, interest was likely to always be a modest sum, but for larger awards of compensation, the imposition of a contractual rate of interest may be significant for lenders.

Settlement Agreements

Holyoake v Candy [2017] EWHC 3397

Unfairness arising in a compromise agreement

Holyoake v Candy marked a significant shift in the applicable principles for parties entering full and final settlement agreements. Before *Holyoake*, consent agreements were generally seen as conclusively binding, except in cases involving mistake or a material change of circumstances. In *Holyoake*, Nugee J undertook an analysis of a 'Settlement Deed' that provided for payment by instalments.

The claimant, Mr Holyoake, was a property developer who brought a claim against six defendants including brothers Nicholas and Christian Candy, and CPC Group Limited ('CPC'), a company ostensibly owned by Christian Candy. The claimant had entered into an unsecured loan agreement with CPC to finance the purchase of a development property. The value of the loan was £12 million. The unfair relationship provisions applied to the loan.

The parties had entered into a settlement deed in relation to claims made by the claimant relating to various consumer credit complaints arising prior to the date of the deed. The terms of the settlement deed were expressed to be on the basis of full and final settlement. The claimant advanced a case that the settlement deed was itself a credit agreement or a related agreement within the meaning of the CCA 1974.

In opposition to the claim, it was argued *inter alia* that the settlement deed was neither a credit agreement nor a related agreement and so could not itself be reopened under the CCA, and that the settlement deed represented a bona fide settlement of the CCA claims which could not, or should not be reopened.

The court rejected the submission that the settlement deed was not a credit agreement on account of the deed not itself providing any financial accommodation.[63] The settlement deed extended time for repayment of the debt which the court found was 'clearly' the provision of "financial accommodation" and hence "credit". The settlement deed was held to be a credit agreement itself.

In any event, the court found that the settlement deed was also a related agreement. At paragraph [499] it was stated:

> *"...By s. 140C(4) an agreement is "related" to a credit agreement (the "main agreement") if, among other things, it is a "linked transaction" in relation to the main agreement; by s. 140C(5) in the case of a credit agreement which is not a regulated consumer credit agreement, a transaction is treated as a linked transaction in relation to that agreement if it would have been had the agreement been a regulated one; and by s.19, a transaction is a linked transaction in relation to a regulated agreement, among other things, if it is an agreement entered into by the debtor with the creditor, the creditor initiated the transaction by suggesting it to the debtor, and the debtor enters into it for a purpose related to the principal agreement: see s. 19(1)(c)(ii), (2)(a). That rather tortuous definition seems to me to be satisfied here: the Settlement Deed was an agreement entered into by Holyoake with CPC; it was initiated by CPC (Mr Dean and Mr Christian Candy*

63 See *Holyoake v Candy* at paragraph 498

> *having told Mr Holyoake the agreements had to be cleansed); and Mr Holyoake entered into it for a purpose related to the principal agreement, namely to obtain CPC's agreement to the Second Supplemental Extension Agreement (which was itself a credit agreement). The Settlement Deed was therefore a linked transaction and a related agreement."*

Regarding the argument that the settlement deed was a bona fide agreement, the court identified an *"obvious danger in holding that any agreement settling CCA claims is effective to oust the Court's powers under ss. 140A-C of the CCA, as it would open the way to lenders routinely requiring borrowers to settle any possible CCA claims, which would run the risk... of driving the proverbial coach and horses through the protection afforded by the CCA."*[64]

The court proceeded on the basis that there was no jurisdictional bar to considering whether the unfairness arose from the relationship arising from the settlement deed.

Despite this finding, the court went on to say at [504]:

> *"On the other hand that does not mean the Settlement Deed is just to be ignored as if it did not exist... the policy of the Court to encourage good faith compromises, and to enforce compromises when they are made – seem to me to continue to apply."*

The Court considered whether a bona fide compromise had been reached on legal advice and if it was, considered it should be slow to go behind it.[65]

Ultimately, the court found that the settlement deed was a bona fide compromise, and the court declined to reopen it.

64 See *Holyoake v Candy* at [501]

65 See *Holyoake v Candy* at [504]

It was further argued in *Holyoake* that in relation to the period after entry into the settlement deed, an unfair relationship arose owing to extension fees of £2.5m that were applied to the loan account. Mr Holyoake had requested the loan extensions himself and if he had not agreed to pay the extension fees, the loan would have been effectively called in and made payable immediately.

Nugee J was referred to *Khodari v Tamimi* [2008] CTLC 269. In that case the claimant had charged a 10% fee to a gambler. The fee was said to reflect the credit risk, rather than the time value of the money.

The court in *Holyoake* declined to hold that *Khodari* was authority that the court's role was not to regulate large returns, or that the mere size of a charge could not by itself give rise to an unfair relationship.[66] On the contrary, it was said that charging a fee that was out of line with industry norms *could* by itself be unfair.

It was noted by Nugee J that the extension fees were high, each extension had been for only a month or so, and that there was no rationale for their calculation. The difficulty for Mr Holyoake was that he was a sophisticated borrower seeking to profit from a business venture. He was securing the opportunity to continue to try to achieve a sale. CPC had correctly judged the price that Mr Holyoake would find it commercially worthwhile to pay.

In holding that no unfairness arose from the imposition of extension fees, it was stated by Nugee J at [524] that:

> *"I do not think the CCA was in general intended to enable the Court to intervene in what is effectively a commercial negotiation between parties who are well able to look after themselves."*

66 See *Holyoake v Candy* at [517]

Self v Santander Cards UK Ltd [2024] EWCA Civ 1106

Fairness of settlement agreements

Self v Santander considered a common argument raised by claimants in PPI claims when lenders rely on a defence of compromise following an offer and acceptance of compensation calculated under the FCA redress scheme.

The Court of Appeal set out to answer the following question:

> *Did the settlement agreements exclude the court's jurisdiction under sections 140A and 140B of the CCA?*

The Court of Appeal adopted and endorsed the approach taken in *Holyoake v Candy*, confirming that the court retains jurisdiction to consider questions of unfairness and redress under sections 140A and 140B of the CCA 1974, even in circumstances where parties have compromised any claims they might have under those sections.

A settlement agreement does not act as a jurisdictional bar to the court considering whether the relationship was unfair, but such an agreement will not simply be ignored either. The terms of the settlement agreement would be considered in determining whether the relationship was unfair. If the terms were found to be fair and reasonable, the settlement agreement should bind the parties unless the compromise was not *bona fide*.

A broad approach should be taken to determine whether a *bona fide* compromise has been reached on legal advice, and if so, the court should be very slow to go behind it.

The Court of Appeal added that it is a matter for the court to determine what weight (if any) to attribute to particular factors as they apply to the facts of the case.

Two factors were, however, considered to be highly relevant:

(i) the complexity and clarity of the terms of the proposed compromise and its consequences; and

(ii) whether the party has access to any necessary advice on the proposed compromise from people other than lawyers.

The court held that the settlement agreements in *Self v Santander* were *bona fide,* and that the terms of the settlement agreements were fair and reasonable. Accordingly, the relationship was not unfair for the purposes of s.140A CCA 1974.

Commercial Loans – Interest Rates, Receivers and Other Considerations

Many of the commonplace allegations of unfairness relate to consumer agreements such as credit cards, store cards, online shopping accounts, and modest personal loans. However, unfair relationship claims also appear in high-value commercial loan disputes, and the number of litigated cases is on the rise.

When assessing unfairness, the court is likely to be slower to find an unfair relationship in the context of high value lending between commercial parties.[67]

The summary of the matters considered relevant to deciding whether there was an unfair relationship by reference to each of the three categories listed in paragraphs (a) – (c) of Section140 (1) given in *Deutsche Bank (Suisse) SA v Khan* [2013] EWHC 482 at [346] is useful:

"(1) In relation to the fairness of the terms themselves:

67 See *Holyoake v Candy* at [508]

a. whether the term is commonplace and/or in the nature of the product in question;

b. whether there are sound commercial reasons for the term;

c. whether it represents a legitimate and proportionate attempt by the creditor to protect its position;

d. to the extent that a term is solely for the benefit of the lender, whether it exists to protect him from a risk which the debtor does not face;

e. the scale of the lending and whether it was commercial or quasi-commercial in nature (a court is likely to be slower to find unfairness in high value lending arrangements between commercial parties than in credit agreements affecting consumers); an

f. the strength (or otherwise) of the debtors bargaining position;

g. whether the terms have been individually negotiated or are pro forma terms and, if so, whether they have been presented on a "take it or leave it" basis;

(2) In relation to the creditor's conduct before and at the time of formation:

a. whether the creditor applied any pressure on the borrowers to execute the agreement (if an agreement has been entered into with a sense of urgency it will be relevant to consider to what extent responsibility for this lay with the debtor, as distinct from the creditor);

b. whether the creditor understood and had reasonable grounds to believe that the borrower had experience of the relevant arrangements and had available to him the advice of solicitors;

c. whether the creditor had any reason to think that the debtor had not read or understood the terms; and

d. whether the debtor demurred at the time of formation over the terms he now suggests are unfair (this point has particular force if he did complain over other terms.

(3) In relation to the creditor's conduct following formation and leading up to enforcement:

a. whether any demand was prompted by an "improper motive" or was the consequence of an "arbitrary decision";

b. whether the creditor has shown patience and, before leaping to enforcement, has taken steps in the hope of reaching some form of accommodation (for example by attending meetings, engaging in correspondence and/or inviting proposals); and

c. whether the debtor has resisted attempts at accommodation by raising unfounded claims against the creditor."

Interest Rates

Seculink Limited v Eren Salih [2023] EWHC 1706 (KB)

High default interest rate

Seculink had obtained an £850,000.00 judgment against Mr Salih pursuant to a secured bridging loan agreement. Mr Justice Soole heard Mr Salih's appeal against the Judge's rejection of (i) his defence that the provision for payment of interest upon default (12% per month compounded) was unenforceable as a penalty, and (ii) his defence and counterclaim that there was an unfair relationship within the meaning of ss.140A-D CCA 1974.

Mr Salih owned three investment properties, each being subject to a mortgage. Seculink loaned Mr Salih the sum of £355,000 to be repaid at the end of a six-month term. Simple interest accrued at a rate of 2.5% per month. In default of redemption at the conclusion of the six-month term, the interest rate on the outstanding sum increased to 12% per month compounded. The loan was secured by way of second legal charge on each of the three properties.

The loan was not redeemed as contractually required and Seculink brought three separate claims against Mr Salih seeking possession of the secured properties and a money judgment.

The claim was defended largely on the basis that the default interest rate (equating to 289.6% per annum) was void as a penalty, and that an unfair relationship arose.

As at the date of trial, Seculink had agreed to limit the value of its claim to £850,000.00, rather than pursuing the actual contractual debt totalling £13.3 million.

At trial, the judge concluded that it was not technically necessary to consider Mr Salih's claims of 'penalties' and unfairness on the basis that both required supporting evidence which had not been provided. Possession of the three properties was ordered and judgment for the debt was entered. Mr Salih's appeal against the decision was allowed.

In relation to the initial rejection of the unfair relationship claim, it was said:

> *"61. I also conclude that the Judge was wrong to reject the claim of unfair relationship on the basis that he did, namely that Mr Salih had provided no evidence on the matter.*
>
> *62. First, this takes no account of the reverse burden of proof: s.140B(9). On the assumption, but without deciding, that there is an evidential burden on the borrower (cf. the discussion in Goldhill*

> *Finance Ltd v. Smyth [2023] EWHC 362 (KB) at [79]-[81] and [118]), this was discharged at least to the extent that Mr Salih contended that the default rate of interest was too high.*
>
> *63. Secondly, as Mr Hope accepts, the Judge was wrong to hold that a challenge to that rate (or indeed to the initial rate of interest) could not succeed without expert evidence in support. Of course, and depending on the particular facts and circumstances, one or other party may fail if it does not call expert evidence; but it does not necessarily fail without it."*

The possession orders and money judgment were set aside, and the issues of penalty and unfair relationship were remitted to the county court for re-trial.

Kumar v LSC Finance Limited [2023] EWHC 1439 (Ch)

High interest rate, promises reneged on by lender, refusal to allow a drawdown, unfair appointment of receivers, sale of property at an undervalue

Kumar is a notable case involving short-term, high interest commercial loans. This case concerned a number of unregulated loan agreements, guarantees and indemnities entered into by Mr Kumar with LSC Finance Limited. One of the many claims advanced by Mr Kumar was unfairness arising from a number of allegations which can be summarised as follows:[68]

- Mr Kumar was re-assured that the date for repayment of some of the loans would be extended beyond 12 months as LSC was aware that Mr Kumar would require more than 12 months to complete intended building work;

68 See *Kumar v LSC Finance Limited* [2023] EWHC 1439 (Ch) at [44]

- LSC refused to allow further drawdown of monies under certain loan agreements causing delay in completion of the building work. There were no proper grounds for such refusal;

- LSC unfairly appointed Receivers to take possession of and sell the secured land;

- LSC allowed the secured land to be sold at an undervalue; and

- the contractual interest payable under certain loan agreements was compound interest of 3% per month.

There was no suggestion that any of the matters complained of could not found a cause of action under the unfair relationship provisions. The court heard evidence and argument on all of the matters alleged.

The allegation that Mr Kumar was re-assured that the date for repayment of some of the loans would be extended beyond 12 months was rejected factually, and the argument that receivers were appointed unfairly was not upheld on the basis that LSC were entitled to take such action.

Regarding the allegation that the receivers sold the secured land at an undervalue, the court took the view that the value of land depended upon what purchasers with the funds to pay for a property were willing to pay for it. There was an alleged difference of £38,000 between the valuation relied upon by Mr Kumar and the sale price achieved. The court held that in the absence of any case that the receivers failed to take reasonable steps to obtain proper market value, it could not conclude that there had been any sale at an undervalue or that LSC had permitted the same.

The allegation that unfairness arose as a result of the speed at which LSC demanded full repayment of the loans after the contractual date of repayment passed, and thereafter appointed receivers was not found to give rise to an unfair relationship for the following reasons set out at [236]:

a) *Mr Kumar had, according to his e mail of 11 August 2018, been attempting to sell the secured Land himself, he provided no evidence that he had achieved any success in doing so;*

b) *it appeared that Mr Kumar was, broadly contemporaneously with seeking a purchaser for the Land, and also seeking to refinance the Loans and, having obtained an offer of refinance the offer did not proceed;*

c) *by the time that LSC issued its demand and proceeded to appoint Receivers, Mr Kumar had been attempting to both sell the land and arrange a refinance for several months but without success. There was no evidence that LSC was unwilling to accept a sale of the Land or a refinance that repaid the Loans;*

d) *the Receivers gave Mr Kumar 3 months from the date of LSC's demand to refinance the Loans and thereafter withdrew the Land from auction, at least on one occasion, to allow Mr Kumar time to fund a purchase of the Land; and*

e) *The court was satisfied that Mr Kumar was allowed a fair opportunity, taking into account the time he had both before and after demand and the appointment of Receivers to repay his Loan, but he was unable, for whatever reasons to do so, and that, in those circumstances, the making of demand and appointment of Receivers did not give rise to an unfair relationship between Mr Kumar and LSC.*

The standard rate of interest payable under the loan agreements was 1.2% per month. In the event that the loans were not redeemed by their due date, interest was payable at 3% per month on the outstanding balance of the loan, compounded.

At [229], and having considered a number of authorities, the court set out its own summary of the factors that were relevant when deciding whether a relationship is unfair because of the interest rate charged:

a) whether the interest rate charged was clear on the face of the loan documents;

b) whether the debtor obtain legal advice before entering into the loan agreement;

c) the sophistication of the debtor and in particular whether they should be taken to understand the terms relating to interest contained in the loan agreement;

d) whether the rate of interest was so high that it was unfair, even if the debtor was aware of and understood its terms; and

e) hoe the interest rate compared to the market rate for similar loans.

The court held that the default interest rate 3% per month compounded was not sufficiently high to mean that the relationship between LSC and the defendants would be unfair. The court did not have any evidence before it as to what the normal or market default interest rate may be in relation to bridging loans yet the court was not prepared to declare any unfairness arising in circumstances where the borrower was aware of the rate and the circumstances in which it would be charged.

LSC's refusing to allow further drawdown of monies under some of the loan agreements was factually proven and was held to give rise to an unfair relationship[69] given that the refusal was not justified either contractually or otherwise. The court was not satisfied that Mr Kumar had sustained any financial loss as a result of the refusal to allow a drawdown on the loan but, as noted at [251], *"Section 140B* is not... *restricted to compensating the consumer for loss they have suffered... Loss suffered by the borrower would nonetheless, in my judgment be necessary to justify a substantial remedy."*

[69] See *Kumar v LSC* at [231]

The court ordered the debt owed by Mr Kumar to be reduced by £13,500 as at a specified date.

Arthistory Ltd v Campbell [2022] EWHC 848 (Ch)

High interest rates, unfair contract terms, failure to honour pre-contract promises

The claimant property company sought specific performance of an agreement granting it an option to acquire the defendants' property and/or for an order that the defendants execute a property transfer to give effect to the option.

The defendants were an elderly couple whose home was due to be repossessed by their mortgagee. Wishing to stay in the property, they entered into a number of agreements with the claimant property company. Under a facility agreement, the claimant loaned £123,215.00 to the defendants to be repaid within 36 months. The loan sums were used to redeem the mortgage. A second legal charge was executed against the property.

If the loan was not redeemed as required, an initial interest rate of 28% per annum would become payable, as well as default interest at an additional 2.5% per month.

An arrangement fee equivalent to 15% of the facility and an exit fee of 3% were also payable.

The parties also entered into an option agreement which, if exercised, the sale of the property would be subject to the continued occupation of the defendants under a tenancy agreement. The option would lapse if not exercised within three years.

Additionally, there was a buy-back option agreement, under which the defendants could purchase the property for an amount equal to the sums outstanding under the facility agreement and legal charge together with certain additions to the price depending on when the option was exercised.

The claimant exercised the option in October 2015.

The claim was defended on the basis that there had been no discussion about an option to purchase the property and that the defendants had signed the agreements in order to stop the property from being repossessed. The defendants alleged that they had challenged some of the terms in the draft documents at the time of execution, and the claimant had told them that the terms would be adjusted and confirmed in a side letter, which was never provided. An unfair relationship was alleged.

The court held that the terms of the loan agreement, taken as a whole, were unfair. The agreement provided for an initial rate of interest of 28% and there was an exit fee of 3%, but it had always been intended that those terms would be waived by the promised side letter.

The Court also found unfairness in relation to the option agreement that had been entered into as it went well beyond what was intended to be security for the facility. It was stated:[70]

> *"Whilst the claimant had sought to justify the option agreement on the basis that the property was worth only £375,000, the evidence suggested that it might be worth significantly more. There were no sound commercial reasons for the option agreement, nor did it represent a legitimate and proportionate attempt by the claimant to protect its position. There was no special risk which the claimant had faced as a result of the facility. Also, there had never been any real prospect of the defendants being able to afford the buy-back option. They had been driven to seek the arrangement with the claimant because of their*

[70] See *Arthistory Ltd v Campbell* at [82-86] and [88]

mortgagee's insistence on re-finance and there had been no viable alternative on offer"

By way of remedy, the option agreement, the buy-back option and the transfers were set aside. The facility agreement and the legal charge remained in place as they provided the secured lending which was the core bargain intended by the parties. The terms of those agreements were, however, altered so as to remove the provision for initial interest at 28% and to remove the 3% exit fee. The arrangement fee of 15% was considered excessive and was replaced with a fee of 10%.[71]

Campbell v Tyrell [2022] EWHC 423 (Ch)

High interest rate, unfair redemption fee, conduct of appointed receivers

In *Campbell*, the Court declined to find any unfairness arising from the conduct of appointed receivers, an interest rate of 2% per calendar month, and a redemption fee of £115,000.00. Whilst the allegations of unfairness regarding the interest rate and the redemption fee had not, in fact, been pleaded, the matters were nonetheless addressed.

The default interest rate was also not held to be unfair, with the Court stating at [102] that:

> *"The default rate is less than twice the primary rate, and it would not have been incurred had the loan been repaid after six months, following a sale of the property. I find nothing unfair in that in view of the increased risks that any default in repayment of a loan inevitably brings."*

---

[71] Additional remedies were awarded to the defendants that are not noted herein.

A redemption fee of £115,000.00 was also not unfair in circumstances where the fee had been negotiated down from £215,000.00 and the borrowers had received independent legal advice.

Kerrigan v Elevate Credit International Ltd (t/a Sunny) [2020] EWHC 2169 (Comm)

High interest rate, failure to undertake proper credit worthiness

The agreement in *Kerrigan* involved regulated credit agreements that were both high cost and short term. The interest rate was 29% per month.

His Honour Judge Worster (sitting as a Judge of the High Court) stated at [198]:

> *"Given that I do not intend working through the issue of relief in the individual cases, it may assist if I summarise the factors that I have found relevant to unfairness when considering the interest rate (and any other charges).*
>
> *(i) First there is the absolute level of the rate. I do regard 29% per month as very high. I appreciate that this is a high risk market for lenders, and the overall return has to justify the overall risk of lending. But that is not an answer in the individual case.*
>
> *(ii) Secondly the relative rate... the court should look at the market rate. This is to include charges so that the real costs rather than the headline interest rate is considered.*
>
> *(iii) Thirdly, where the borrower was "fully aware" of the rate. No HCST borrower is going to have the benefit of legal advice, but HHJ Cooke's approach in Chubb reflects an important point. A rate which is high may not lead to an unfair relationship if the borrower knows or ought to know the bargain they are making, but the position may be*

> *different if they do not. Here it is relevant to look at how the rates are presented to the borrower in the course of the application process. The Defendant does quite a good job. The use of the tick box without the need to scroll down and the fact that none of the claimants reads the terms is a worry. But the overall cost of this borrowing is made plain.*
>
> *(iv) Fourthly the potential for the borrower to suffer harm, particularly when that is something which was or ought to be known by the lender. Higher rates are likely to create a greater risk of harm for those who are marginally eligible. That in turn will affect the fairness of the relationship.*
>
> *That is not an exhaustive list, and there may be other matters which arise in individual cases. The Claimants do not suggest that any unfairness arises from any of the other terms."*

Kerrigan also notably stated at [11] that:

> *"... a failure by a creditor to undertake a proper creditworthiness assessment prior to entering into a regulated credit agreement would almost certainly affect the fairness of the relationship and so trigger the Court's powers to make appropriate orders under section 140B."*

Notting Hill Finance Ltd. v. Hussein **[2019] EWCA Civ 1337**

High default interest rate

In *Notting Hill Finance*, a default interest rate of 12% per month to be compounded was considered, albeit in the context of whether it was right to allow the issues of penalty and unfair relationship to be raised as new points on an appeal.

At [45] Snowden J (as he then was) observed:

> *'In the instant case, the default interest rate of 289.6% per annum was, on any view, remarkably high for a secured loan... It was also apparent*

that the mortgage debt on a scheduled payment on maturity of £71,000 was claimed to have risen by over £20,000 in the space of a little over six weeks between the issue of proceedings and the hearing. Those numbers are sufficiently striking but I would have expected them to have rung alarm-bells for the District Judge, even given his busy list. Whilst I do not express any view as to whether the District Judge was under any positive duty to do so, in my view he could not possibly have been criticised if he had raised the issue of whether such a term was penal or unfair to the Defendant of his own motion.'

Greenlands Trading Ltd v Pontearso [2019] EWHC 278 (Ch)

High standard interest rate and default interest rate

Under the agreement entered into between Greenlands Trading and Pontearso, the applicable standard contractual rate of interest was 1.45% per month. A default interest rate of 3% per month would apply in the event of breach. Nugee J, applying the considerations in *Chubb v Dean* stated at [55] to [57]:

'These sorts of considerations – the fact that the rate was clear and not buried in small print, that the borrowers knew what they were doing and were legally advised, that they were intelligent consumers and not misled – seem to me to be precisely the sort of considerations which were likely among other things to be relevant to the assessment of whether a relationship is unfair by virtue of a particular term and to have foreshadowed in advance, as it were the list of matters which Lord Sumption specifically refers to at [17] of Plevin:

"... the characteristics of the borrower, her sophistication or vulnerability, the facts which she could reasonably be expected to know or assume, the range of choices available to her, and the degree to which the creditor was and should have been aware of these matters."

In this case too, the judge found as facts – and it has not been suggested that he was wrong to do so – not only that the defendant was legally advised ... but also that ....:

"She appears to know her own mind and is certainly not naïve when it comes to lending and mortgages, albeit that she may not have taken out a bridging loan before these two bridging loans. She knew that they were short term loans which had to be repaid."

And, ... he found that the defendant told her solicitor that she was a businesswoman, and that although he explained it was a bridging loan and was risky "she was very keen to get the loan"; that she had significant property assets; and that "on her own evidence" ... "she knew that the interest rate and other charges were high" and she "was experienced in mortgaging properties to raise funds and appears to have had some knowledge of the lending industry, changing mortgage providers for a better interest rate. She has a number of properties and was certainly not naïve or unsophisticated.'

Chubb v Dean [2013] EWHC 1282 (Ch)

High interest rate – no unfairness found

A contractual interest rate of 1.85% and a facility fee of 1.25% were expressly waived under the terms of the agreement if the loan was repaid in full by its due date. The court considered the rate of interest to be 'high', but no unfairness arose as a result. His Honour Judge Cooke (sitting as a High Court Judge) stated at [26]:

"In the case of the two provisions that are at issue here by virtue of the master's order, it seems to me that individually and particularly together they impose a high charge at a high rate for the use of this facility but it is a rate that is clear on the face of the documents. It cannot be said to be buried in small print. It is there to be seen on the face of the documents in very legible print and something that can be

clearly evaluated by somebody entering into those documents. In the present case, the defendants were legally advised. There is a separate certificate of a solicitor to the effect that he has advised them upon the contents of the document they were signing. Mr Dean is himself a lawyer, a barrister in private practice although not in the civil field. He and his wife are clearly intelligent consumers and able both to read and understand the documents themselves and to absorb the effect of the advice that they were given. They, therefore, must be taken to have known the bargain that they have made, and it seems to me they cannot say, and have not sought to say, that they were in any way misled by the documentation or did not understand what they were signing up for. The rate of interest, whether one adds the facility fee to it or not, is high. It is not, however, it seems to me, even in combination so high that it would lead the court to the conclusion that the relationship between the two parties to such an agreement was unfair even if the consumer was fully aware of all the terms he was entering into. There may, of course, be such cases but it seems to me that they would require a very much higher interest rate than even the combination of these two amounts gives rise to in this case. What the defendants signed up to was a stiff commercial bargain no doubt but it was not, in my judgment, an unfair one, and the relationship it created was not unfair by virtue of those terms."

Issues of Conduct

Credit Capital Corp Ltd v Watson [2021] EWHC 466 (QB)

Fee paid to broker, interest clauses, conduct of the lender, sale of property at an undervalue

In this case the defendant had defaulted on the repayment terms of a bridging loan. An allegation of unfair relationship was made but rejected by the court.

Regarding a fee paid by the lender to the broker, it was found that the evidence did not suggest that the broker had stopped acting for the borrower as alleged, or that the broker fee had not been properly paid. The lender was entitled to pay the broker and charge the fee to the borrower (at [64]).

The loan agreement included a clause that permitted the lender to withhold 12 months' worth of interest payments while still charging interest on the withheld amount. This clause was not found to be unfair. The clause was justified as it had been negotiated in a commercial context and with the benefit of legal advice (at [67]).

The debtor alleged unfairness based on the lender's conduct in having appointed LPA receivers and expressing dissatisfaction with the debtor's position. It was held that no unfairness arose, that the lender was entitled to take the action that it did, and the use of forceful language did not by itself give rise to an unfair relationship (at [77]).

There was no evidence to establish that property had been sold at an undervalue, so this element of the claim failed on its facts. There was also no evidence of an absence of good faith on the part of the LPA receiver regarding the fact that the property had not been sold. The court confirmed that the lender was not liable for the acts and defaults of the receiver unless it gave directions to the receiver or it interfered with the receiver's conduct. There was no evidence of that (at [103-106]).

Clydesdale Bank Plc (t/a Yorkshire Bank) v Wardle [2020] EWHC 82 (Ch)

Failure to explain partnership liability

The relationship between a bank and a partnership had been unfair where the lender had offered a partnership loan with a 10-year fixed interest term without providing a sufficient explanation as to the partnership's liability for potentially substantial break costs in the event of early repayment. It was a feature of the case that the partnership would have agreed a shorter fixed rate period if an appropriate explanation had been given.

The court applied the following approach in light of considered authorities:

- Section 140A is highly dependent upon the individual circumstances of the debtor and the particular relationship between the creditor and the debtor. It must be assessed from the perspective of the relationship as a whole.

- In order to conclude that the relationship is unfair it is necessary to identify a particular attribute of the relationship that is unfair.

- If that attribute would, but for limitation, give rise to a standalone cause of action, then it can only give rise to unfairness if the necessary elements of that standalone cause of action are made out.

- Causation has a critical part to play in the analysis: a particular matter raised by a debtor cannot make the relationship unfair if it had no causal impact.

- In considering the fairness or otherwise of a particular transaction and the relationship between creditor and debtor, it is important to consider the position at the time the transaction was entered into and not to be influenced by hindsight.

Goldhill Finance Ltd v Berry [2018] 10 WLUK 480 – County Court decision

Conduct of lender

In this case, the lender took possession of a property one day after the court had ordered a suspension of the warrant of eviction. An unfair relationship was found as a result.

When considering what order to make, the court considered the borrower's failure to engage with the lender in relation to repayment; her failure to respond to the court proceedings until very late in the day; her attempts to delay matters; the fact that the lender had acted in defiance of a court order; the fact that the lender was acting on advice and was not deliberately acting improperly; the lender's failure to tell the tenants that the warrant had been suspended; and the fact that the borrower was deprived of the opportunity to complete the sale.

An order would be made on the basis that the borrower's planned sale would have completed on 16 September 2016. The lender would receive £40,100, being the shortfall on that date. The lender was also entitled to contractual interest at the default rate until trial.

Terms of the Agreement

***Pilgrim Rock Ltd v Iwaniuk* [2019] EWHC 203 (Ch)**

Terms of the agreement, high interest rate

When this case was heard unfairness was found in the terms of the agreement and the fact that the lender had done nothing to enforce its rights for four years while interest was accruing at an escalated rate. Further, interest increased after the agreement had come to term, and the rate of interest was onerous in comparison to terms that would have been obtainable on the open market.

Judgment was given in favour of the lender for the capital sum and interest, but the terms of the loan agreement were varied to reduce the rate of interest, to provide for interest compounding annually rather than quarterly and to lengthen the term or repayment date thereby limiting the period for which default interest could be charged.

Statutory Breaches

***Carey and others -v- HSBC and others*, OFT intervening [2009] EWHC 3417 (QB)**

Non-compliance with statutory obligations

In *Carey v HSBC*, the High Court considered the extent of a creditor's obligations under section 78 of the Consumer Credit Act 1974, and whether a failure to comply with those obligations could render the credit relationship "unfair" under section 140A.

The claimants had argued that the creditors' failure to provide an original, signed copy of the credit agreement in response to a section 78 request rendered the agreements unenforceable and gave rise to an unfair relationship. The court rejected this argument.

The court held that non-compliance with section 78 does not automatically result in an unfair relationship. To establish unfairness under section 140A, the debtor must demonstrate more than just a technical breach or procedural failing; there must be substantive evidence of unfair conduct or treatment by the creditor.

The judgment made clear that the concept of an unfair relationship is fact-sensitive, and it is not enough to rely on technicalities or hypothetical prejudice. A debtor seeking to argue unfairness must show real detriment or an imbalance in the relationship that goes beyond a mere delay or defect in document provision.

'The Electronic Communications Code: A Practical Guide – Second Edition' by Kerry Bretherton KC, James Castle, Mark Loveday
'A Practical Guide to the Independent School Standards – September 2023 Edition' by Sarah McKimm
'A Practical Guide to Estate Administration and Crypto Assets' by Richard Marshall
'A Practical Guide to Parental Alienation in Private and Public Law Children Cases' by Sam King QC & Frankie Shama
'Contested Heritage – Removing Art from Land and Historic Buildings' by Richard Harwood QC, Catherine Dobson, David Sawtell
'The Limits of Separate Legal Personality: When Those Running a Company Can Be Held Personally Liable for Losses Caused to Third Parties Outside of the Company' by Dr Mike Wilkinson
'A Practical Guide to Transgender Law' by Robin Moira White & Nicola Newbegin
'A Practical Guide to 'Stranded Spouses' in Family Law' by Mani Singh Basi
'A Practical Guide to Residential Freehold Conveyancing' by Lorraine Richardson
'A Practical Guide to Pensions on Divorce for Lawyers' by Bryan Scant
'A Practical Guide to Challenging Sham Marriage Allegations in Immigration Law' by Priya Solanki
'A Practical Guide to Digital Communications Evidence in Criminal Law' by Sam Willis
'A Practical Guide to Legal Rights in Scotland' by Sarah-Jane Macdonald
'A Practical Guide to New Build Conveyancing' by Paul Sams & Rebecca East
'A Practical Guide to Inherited Wealth on Divorce' by Hayley Trim
'A Practical Guide to Practice Direction 12J and Domestic Abuse in Private Law Children Proceedings' by Rebecca Cross & Malvika Jaganmohan
'A Practical Guide to Confiscation and Restraint' by Narita Bahra QC, John Carl Townsend, David Winch
'A Practical Guide to the Law of Forests in Scotland' by Philip Buchan
'A Practical Guide to Health and Medical Cases in Immigration Law' by Rebecca Chapman & Miranda Butler
'A Practical Guide to Bad Character Evidence for Criminal Practitioners by Aparna Rao
'A Practical Guide to Extradition Law post-Brexit' by Myles Grandison et al
'A Practical Guide to Hoarding and Mental Health for Housing Lawyers' by Rachel Coyle

'Stephens on Contractual Indemnities' by Richard Stephens
'A Practical Guide to the EU Succession Regulation' by Richard Frimston
'A Practical Guide to Solicitor and Client Costs – Second Edition' by Robin Dunne
'Constructive Dismissal – Practice Pointers and Principles' by Benjimin Burgher
'A Practical Guide to Religion and Belief Discrimination Claims in the Workplace' by Kashif Ali
'A Practical Guide to the Law of Medical Treatment Decisions' by Ben Troke
'Fundamental Dishonesty and QOCS in Personal Injury Proceedings: Law and Practice' by Jake Rowley
'A Practical Guide to the Law in Relation to School Exclusions' by Charlotte Hadfield & Alice de Coverley
'A Practical Guide to Divorce for the Silver Separators' by Karin Walker
'The Right to be Forgotten – The Law and Practical Issues' by Melissa Stock
'A Practical Guide to Planning Law and Rights of Way in National Parks, the Broads and AONBs' by James Maurici QC, James Neill et al
'A Practical Guide to Election Law' by Tom Tabori
'A Practical Guide to the Law in Relation to Surrogacy' by Andrew Powell
'A Practical Guide to Claims Arising from Fatal Accidents – Second Edition' by James Patience
'A Practical Guide to Asbestos Claims' by Jonathan Owen & Gareth McAloon
'A Practical Guide to Stamp Duty Land Tax in England and Northern Ireland' by Suzanne O'Hara
'A Practical Guide to the Law of Farming Partnerships' by Philip Whitcomb
'A Practical Guide to the Law of Unlawful Eviction and Harassment – Second Edition' by Stephanie Lovegrove
'A Practical Guide to Costs in Personal Injury Claims – Second Edition' by Matthew Hoe
'A Practical Guide to the General Data Protection Regulation (GDPR) – Second Edition' by Keith Markham
'A Practical Guide to Working with Litigants in Person and McKenzie Friends in Family Cases' by Stuart Barlow
'Protecting Unregistered Brands: A Practical Guide to the Law of Passing Off' by Lorna Brazell
'A Practical Guide to Secondary Liability and Joint Enterprise Post-Jogee' by Joanne Cecil & James Mehigan

'A Practical Guide to the Pre-Action RTA Claims Protocol for Personal Injury Lawyers' by Antonia Ford
'A Practical Guide to Neighbour Disputes and the Law' by Alexander Walsh
'A Practical Guide to Coercive Control for Legal Practitioners and Victims' by Rachel Horman
'A Practical Guide to the Law of Driverless Cars – Second Edition'
by Alex Glassbrook, Emma Northey & Scarlett Milligan
'A Practical Guide to TOLATA Claims' by Greg Williams
'A Practical Guide to Elderly Law – Second Edition' by Justin Patten
'A Practical Guide to Responding to Housing Disrepair and Unfitness Claims' by Iain Wightwick
'A Practical Guide to the Law of Bullying and Harassment in the Workplace' by Philip Hyland
'How to Be a Freelance Solicitor: A Practical Guide to the SRA-Regulated Freelance Solicitor Model' by Paul Bennett
'A Practical Guide to Prison Injury Claims' by Malcolm Johnson
'A Practical Guide to Advising Clients at the Police Station' by Colin Stephen McKeown-Beaumont
'A Practical Guide to Antisocial Behaviour Injunctions – Second Edition' by Iain Wightwick
'Practical Mediation: A Guide for Mediators, Advocates, Advisers, Lawyers, and Students in Civil, Commercial, Business, Property, Workplace, and Employment Cases' by Jonathan Dingle with John Sephton
'The Mini-Pupillage Workbook' by David Boyle
'A Practical Guide to Crofting Law' by Brian Inkster
'A Practical Guide to the Law of Domain Names and Cybersquatting' by Andrew Clemson
'A Practical Guide to the Law of Gender Pay Gap Reporting' by Harini Iyengar
'NHS Whistleblowing and the Law' by Joseph England
'Employment Law and the Gig Economy' by Nigel Mackay & Annie Powell
'A Practical Guide to Noise Induced Hearing Loss (NIHL) Claims' by Andrew Mckie, Ian Skeate, Gareth McAloon
'An Introduction to Beauty Negligence Claims – A Practical Guide for the Personal Injury Practitioner' by Greg Almond
'Intercompany Agreements for Transfer Pricing Compliance' by Paul Sutton
'Zen and the Art of Mediation' by Martin Plowman
'A Practical Guide to Adoption for Family Lawyers' by Graham Pegg

www.ingramcontent.com/pod-product-compliance
Ingram Content Group UK Ltd.
Pitfield, Milton Keynes, MK11 3LW, UK
UKHW020148290926
15471UKWH00004B/752

9 781916 698932